The Legacy Game Plan

4 Keys to Living Intentionally

Gary Greeno

Testimonials

"Coach Greeno, as I would call him in high school, has the heart and passion to help others strengthen and find their faith. On a daily basis he helped me stay the course and I thank God for his extraordinary leadership!"

- Brandin Cooks, NFL, L.A. Rams Wide Receiver

"In The Legacy Game Plan, Gary lays out the necessary tools to live a meaningful life that impacts others. This book will help you establish your priorities and give you a game plan so that you can seize every moment and live a life of no regrets."

- Ruben Gonzalez, Olympian, Author, Keynote Speaker, www.TheLugeMan.com

"The Legacy Game Plan is a must read for anyone who wants to be intentional about the way they live. The principles Gary has outlined in this book provides a strategy for living out your purpose and impacting as many people as possible. If you want to be a living legacy then this book is for you!"

- Patrick Snow, International Best-Selling Author of Creating Your Own Destiny, www.createyourowndestiny.com

"If you desire to live a life of influence that will be a Godly legacy for future generations read this book! You will discover the power and passion God has instilled in you to make a positive difference in the lives of others."

- Roger Crawford, Hall of Fame Speaker and author of How High Can You Bounce, www.rogercrawford.com

"The Legacy Game Plan is an invaluable resource that will help you develop a personal plan for your life. Gary guides you on a practical journey that promises a more intentional life and the legacy God has for you."

- Dan Reiland, Executive Pastor, 12Stone Church, Lawrenceville, GA

"If you want wisdom gained and proven to work in real life, Gary Greeno's new book is for you."

- Hal Perkins, President of Heartwalk; Author, www.discipledbyjesus.org

"What an excellent, well thought through Book! With your one and only life and your legacy, it is one thing to start well, to stay well, to continue well, and to finish well. Gary not only shares with us how to do that with intentionally, but more than that, he also shares with us how to finish Strong. His illustrations are invaluable!"

- Carl Summer, former District Superintendent, Church of the Nazarene

"Gary is a leader. He's also a lifelong learner always asking questions in order to maximize his impact. This book is a collection of the wisdom he's accumulated over the years that will provide us with the game plan we need in order to be successful wherever we lead from the pulpit to the basketball court. Leading will always make a difference, Gary will help show you how to leave a legacy."

- Pastor John Volinsky, Bayside Church Roseville, CA

"The Legacy Game Plan is a thought-provoking, legacy inspiring, soul-enriching guide towards intentional and purpose-filled living for both the young and old. Having watched Gary' s philosophy on

legacy up close for nearly 7 years, the reader that picks up this book is ensured to be appropriately challenged towards achieving their personal best in both life and faith by someone who has walked the walk."
- **Brandon K. Rachal, Pastor of Preaching & Vision, Redemption City Church, Life Coach and Founder of The Journeymen Discipleship Program. www.mmcmnetwork.com**

"In this book Gary lays the foundation and structure essential for living a fulfilled life today, that will leave a legacy for generations to come. The Legacy Game Plan inspires your vision, challenges your thinking, and empowers you with the tools to make a positive difference."
- **Kevin J Lincoln II, Executive Pastor, LifeSong Church Stockton, CA**

"Inspirational, challenging, and motivational is the way I would describe Gary Greeno's book, *The Legacy Game Plan*. Coach Greeno's game plan for living a life that matters truly challenges you to live intentionally TODAY while being focused on leaving a legacy that will inspire others to do the same! Filled with practical exercises and thought provoking questions this book will not only make you think, it will motivate to you to interact with others as you share what you learn and put it into practice!"
- **CJ Rapp, Speaker and Author, www.CJrapp.com**

"I wish every follower of Jesus would read and follow "The Game Plan" so they can live and leave behind a Godly legacy."
- **Rev. Dr. Earl L. Gillett, Pastor Horizon Christian Fellowship Church of the Nazarene**

GARY GREENO

Join The Facebook Group:
www.facebook.com/groups/LiveYourLegacyWithGaryGreeno

Contents

Acknowledgments

There are many people who have helped make this book possible by having a major influence on my life.

Merwin and Becky Doud have prayed for me, put up with me, and believed in me since I was in the 4th grade. Their Godly influence on me in my formative years has been profound.

Mark Bodenstab invested time in me, never gave up on me, and taught me what it means to follow Christ. I will always be grateful for his influence.

Mark Bernhardt stood by me, listened to me, taught me and spoke truth into my life as a young adult. His commitment to teaching me and discipling me have helped me in many areas of my life.

I am forever grateful for my parents, Ron and Paullette Greeno. One could not find a better example of what it means to live out a Godly legacy. Words can never describe what their love, support, and commitment to me means. Thank you also to my sisters, Pam and Debbie, for their continued love and support that has always been there.

My wife, Dena, has been an incredible support, loving me and growing with me in our faith. I love you.

My children, Bret, Brittney, Brooke, Grace and Luke have each blessed me in many ways. I am so thankful for them and pray that I live in a way that inspires them to live out their own Godly legacy.

Thank you to Chris Johnson, Earl Gillett, and my parents Ron and Paullette for helping me by reading the first manuscripts of this book and offering their feedback and suggestions.

Introduction

"The great use of life is to spend it on something that will outlast it."
– William James

"Life is but a mist, it's like a flower in the field. The wind blows, and we are gone..."
– Psalm 103:15-16 (NLT)

The fact you are reading this book tells me there is something inside of you that wants to squeeze the most possible out of life. You want to make the most out of the time you have on this earth and you are the kind of person who isn't satisfied with the status quo and just drifting through life. You want to make your mark on this world and impact as many people as possible.

I'm writing this book because I want to help you leave a lasting legacy. Our time on this earth is short and it's my hope that this book helps you make the absolute most of it.

The legacy we leave is the legacy we are currently living, so our decisions now must match what we want said about us when we are gone. The way we live today, the choices we make, our behavior, attitudes, and actions each and every day will determine the legacy we leave tomorrow.

Those who have left a great legacy did so because that's what they lived out. The impact of their lives continues to touch and change people long after they are gone.

This is what a great legacy is. It's having an impact and influence on people after you are gone.

The purpose of this book is to help you make choices today that will keep your legacy alive long after you are gone. The greater your impact and influence now while you're alive, the greater your legacy will be.

The Game Plan

I have been a basketball coach for 28 years. When I prepare my team for a game, we always have a game plan. I am very intentional about our strategy to give my team it's best chance to win. I look at all the factors including the strengths and weaknesses of my team, as well as that of our opponent. It is then that I create the game plan. A game plan is important because it gives the team a mission. It provides purpose and organization.

But creating the game plan is only half of it. *Execution* is the other half. Once the coach creates the game plan, it's up to the team to know it and execute it successfully.

When I create the game plan, I always keep in mind that the

opposition has their own game plan, which includes trying to keep us from executing ours. The winning team will not necessarily have a better game plan but will be the one that better *executes* their game plan.

The purpose of this book is to give you a "Game Plan" for leaving a great legacy. I want to help you be intentional about how you live, and help you *develop* and *execute* your own game plan.

I Peter 5:8 tells us,

"Stay alert! Watch out for your great enemy, the devil. He prowls around like a roaring lion, looking for someone to devour." (NLT)

Satan is your opposition and, believe me, he has his own game plan and it includes destroying your legacy.

The good news is that God tells us the victory is ours. Romans 8:37 tells us,

"...despite all these things, overwhelming victory is ours through Christ, who loved us." (NLT)

So, if you carefully craft and execute your game plan, victory is assured. How cool is it to know that victory is guaranteed?

Avoid the Drift

Being intentional is powerful. It provides motivation and gives direction. The opposite of being intentional is drifting. It's a dangerous thing to just drift, being tossed around by the currents of life, having no control over where you are going.

Many years ago, my father and one of his friends took us fishing just off the Oregon coast. We were in his small boat fishing for Rock Cod in amongst the rocks. The fish finder gave us a good location to drop our lines, about 100 yards from the rocks. We were so consumed with what we were doing, we didn't realize we were drifting towards a large boulder in the water.

It was almost too late. As we drifted within feet of the rock, still unaware of what was happening, a wave broke right into the boat, spilling water everywhere. The sudden rush of water into the boat certainly got our attention focused on what really mattered! Fortunately, we were able to get the boat started and move away to a safer place.

Many people live their lives like this. They just drift along, consumed with the moment, unaware they are drifting wherever the currents of life happen to take them. They are consumed with their job, consumed with raising their family, consumed with their finances; they are so focused on just getting through the day they are not being intentional about where their life is headed. Only when the waves of life hit them do they wake up to the reality of their situation.

This book will help you avoid the drift and become intentional with the legacy you want to leave. It's about helping you design your life, rather than just making a living.

Don't drift through life. Live on purpose, for a purpose. After all, this is what God created you for!

There are four parts to the Legacy Game Plan. In this book, I go deep into these four aspects, teaching and illustrating what they are and the significance each has in living out a Godly legacy. The sections are divided into short chapters and at the end of each chapter are questions to help you to develop your own game plan.

The 4 Part Game Plan: Living Out A Godly Legacy
1. Fortify Your Foundation
2. Feed Your Faith
3. Fix Your Focus
4. Finish Strong

Chapter 10 is the culmination of this book. In this chapter, you will create your own game plan by writing out your own:
1. Legacy Statement
2. Legacy Prayer
3. Tombstone Testimony
4. Life Verse

Your Legacy Statement
This is a statement you are going to write about how you will live. It's a statement of declaration that you will read often, reminding you of your daily commitment to live out the legacy you want to leave. Your legacy statement will help you focus and be intentional. I have included my own legacy statement for you as an example but I want you to create your own that is personal and applies specifically to you.

Your Legacy Prayer
Your legacy prayer is a prayer you will write out, asking the Lord to help you live out your legacy statement.

Your Tombstone Testimony

Whenever I attend a funeral and have the chance to walk through a cemetery, I am always fascinated by the tombstones and what's written on them. There is a name, the year the person was born, a dash, and the year the person died. Sometimes there is also something written about the person. There's not a lot of room to write on a tombstone so a tombstone testimony is one brief sentence that sums up your life.

One day, we will breathe our last breath. When you are gone, what will you want people to read about you, in one sentence, that gives them a glimpse into your legacy and what your life was all about? This is your tombstone testimony.

Your Life Verse

There are so many amazing Scriptures that help us exactly where our need is. Do you have a favorite? But more than just a favorite verse, do you have one that you can really take as your promise? That you can cling to through the many challenges of life?

Many years ago, I memorized James 1:12 which says, "Blessed is the one who perseveres under trial, because having stood the test, that person will receive the crown of life that the Lord has promised to those who love him.". Then over the course of the following years, I found great strength and help in these words. I adopted this passage as my "life verse". It's my go-to verse, if you will. If you don't already have such a verse, I would love for you to identify your own go-to verse. I have included a place in the back of the book for you to write out your life verse, along with why it's so important to you. You will come back to this verse time and time again as you navigate through life and live out your legacy.

The Legacy You Leave is The Legacy You Live. Be Intentional!

You have the choice to live out the kind of legacy you want to leave. The decisions you make today will determine the legacy you leave tomorrow. It's not a matter of *will* you leave a legacy, but rather a matter of *what kind* of legacy will you leave? And that is something you can control by how you live today.

To live out the legacy you want to leave you must live intentionally, on purpose. You must decide how you want to live and then decide to live that way every day.

It's Never Too Late

If you're reading this and feel like it's too late, let me tell you, it's never too late. As long as you have breath, you are able to make new decisions to create new results. It may be difficult, but nothing is impossible with God. He forgives the unforgivable, and therefore there is always hope.

"Though you cannot go back in time and create a new beginning, you can start now and create a new ending."
– John Maxwell

"It's never too late to be what you might have been."
– George Eliot

PART 1
Fortify Your Foundation

1

Pass The Baton

*"...if only I may finish the race, and complete the task the Lord
Jesus has given me..."*
– Acts 20:24 (NLT)

What or who do you think of when you hear the word legacy?
Perhaps you think of someone like Billy Graham who recently
passed away. He touched many lives around the world. I doubt
there has been anyone in history to bring as many people to Jesus
as the Reverend Billy Graham did. His legacy continues even
though he is gone and the impact of his life is still affecting others
to this day.

When I think about the word legacy, I think about my grandfather,
John Greeno. He was a Godly man who left a great legacy. He was
a minister, like his dad, my great grandfather. As a family growing
up, we used to gather every year or so for a big family reunion. I'll
never forget one summer in Northern California near Mt. Shasta
when we gathered with the whole family; my grandpa, his four

kids, and many grandkids.

Grandpa was sitting in this big chair in the family room of a large house we had all rented for the week. A few of us were with him, and we began asking him questions about life, and about his relationship with the Lord. As other family members saw what was taking place, they began gathering around to listen to grandpa tell his stories. Someone got out a video camera (this was before cell phones!) as we all understood the significance of the moment.

We were getting a rich experience, listening to a man that we loved, that loved all of us, and that lived his life well.

Grandpa had lived out the legacy he wanted to leave. He taught his children to follow Jesus and they have taught their children to follow him, too, which I am a product of. I am doing everything I can to pass on that legacy to my children, as are my sisters to their children. When John Greeno passed away, he didn't have much worldly wealth, but he had stored up more riches in heaven than could be counted because of how he lived on this earth and how his life impacted those around him, beginning with his family. His legacy and impact continue on, even to this day.

My grandpa ran and finished his race well. Then, my dad took the baton and is leaving me an amazing legacy. He modeled for me everything you are going to read about in this book. He is the greatest man I know.

My dad was a pastor and I'll always remember this one Sunday night when I was growing up, when we still had Sunday Night church services. My dad was concluding his sermon and he had families gather up in a circle while he spoke to them about the importance of our families and making Godly choices. Since my dad was the pastor, my two sisters and I, along with my mom, circled up with my dad on the stage of the large sanctuary at Medford First Church of the Nazarene in Medford, OR. I remember the passion in which my dad spoke and I've had his words ringing in my ear ever since.

He said, "I want my children to say, 'I want the God of my dad to be my God too.'"

My dad was passing the baton of faith to me and in that moment as a young teen I knew I had to grab ahold of it. The calling in my soul screamed my name saying, "Gary! Grab the baton and run!" I haven't run a perfect race by any means, but I'm definitely giving it everything I've got.

My grandpa successfully passed the baton of the faith to my dad. My dad received the baton and is still running an incredible race. He set the example for me and my siblings and showed us how to live. He has shown me how to be a man and has successfully passed that baton on to me. I have taken hold of it and now it's my job to run my race to the best of my ability and pass it on to my kids. And I don't want to drop the baton! I am going to do everything I can to run my race well, just like my grandfather, and father did before me.

You don't have to be a pastor, have a huge platform, or large-scale ministry to run a great race and live out an amazing, Godly legacy. You just have to run! Grab the baton of faith from whoever shared the Gospel with you and go make a difference in your world. Let your life be a living testimony so that you make a positive impact on those around you by influencing how they live. They can then in turn go and do the same with the people they know. This kind of impact is what it means to live out a legacy.

In the 2008 Olympics, the U.S. women's track team was highly favored to win the women's 400-meter relay race. In the semi-final race, the team ran the first three legs well and were looking for a great finish. Unfortunately, as Tori Edwards attempted to pass the baton on to her teammate, Lauren Williams, for the final 100 meters, the exchange was unsuccessful. The baton was dropped. There are pictures of anguish on the face of Williams as she went back to retrieve the baton, pick it up and run across the finish line. Because the baton was dropped, the team was disqualified.

You and I are running a race. You're reading this because you want to make sure you successfully pass the baton of your faith to those who come after you. The good news of the Gospel is that if you drop the baton, you can pick it back up – God does not disqualify you.

A legacy always starts with impacting your family and those closest to you. They are the ones who know the good, the bad, and the ugly about us. Leaving a legacy doesn't mean living a perfect life, it means living a sincere life with pure motives and Godly intentions. It means doing everything we can to make a lasting difference. We will stumble and fall, but failure doesn't have to be fatal, nor does it have to be final.

In I Corinthians 9:24, Paul says,

"Don't you know that in a race all the runners run, but only one

gets the prize. Run in such a way as to get the prize." (NIV)

This is how I want to live! How about you?

Paul Passed the Baton to Timothy

We can learn from the Apostle, Paul about the power of being intentional when it comes to passing the baton. Paul mentored Timothy; he saw something in young Timothy that caused him to want to invest in his life.

In 2 Timothy 1:5, Paul describes Timothy's foundation by saying,

"I am reminded of your sincere faith, which first lived in your grandmother Lois, and in your mother Eunice, and I am persuaded, now lives in you." (NIV)

Timothy's grandmother passed the baton to his mom, who in turn passed it on to him. They left a legacy of faith for Timothy to build his life on and Paul saw that same type of sincere faith in Timothy. Paul says he was persuaded that he had it.

This verse causes me to stop and reflect. When people look at my life, are they persuaded that my life is built on the Word of God? Do they see this same type of sincere faith in me? They saw it in my grandpa. They see it in my dad. I want to live in the same manner, so they see it in me. I want people to look at my children and see it in them.

What about you? Are you living in such a way that people are persuaded that you live for Christ? Do they see in you the legacy you say you want to leave?

Paul goes on to tell Timothy in 2 Timothy 3:14,

"...continue in what you have learned and have become convinced of..." (NIV)

Take note of the two "C" words: *continue* and *convinced*. Paul tells him to continue in what he has learned. In other words, don't stop. Don't give up. You have to keep going with the things you have become convinced of.

This makes me stop to ask, "What are the things that I am really convinced of? What are my convictions, the things that are the non-negotiables in my life?" When you identify those things and make a commitment to continue in them, you will build for a foundation that can withstand the storms and circumstances of life.

If we can continue building our legacy, staying faithful (not perfect, but faithful) then when we get to the end, we can say along with Paul in 2 Timothy 4:7,

"I have fought the good fight, I have finished the race, I have kept the faith." (NIV)

I am very fortunate to have the heritage of a Godly family. If you are blessed to have that too, then make sure you grab that baton and run well!

I meet people all the time, however, that didn't have parents who raised them to be followers of Christ. Maybe you're reading this and you came to know Jesus later in life, or perhaps you don't have a relationship with him now and you're wondering how to even go about that.

If this is you, you have the potential to start something new. You have the ability to steer your family in a Godly direction. A new legacy can start with you. God is so desiring for you to follow Him and serve Him with all your heart; He wants you to be a part of the generation that begins to establish a new legacy. He wants to begin it with you!

Paul gives us a model to follow about leaving a legacy. He lived his life on purpose, for a purpose. He was intentional about mentoring Timothy so that he took ahold of that baton. We can look at Paul and Timothy and see they ran their race well, which is exactly the way we are to run.

Action Points

1. What race are you running? Where will you end up if you stay on this path?

   _____

   _____

   _____

   _____

   _____

   _____

2. Who in your life are you passing the baton of faith to?

   _____

   _____

   _____

   _____

   _____

3. How well are you running your race? Are you being intentional about passing the baton? If not, what changes can you start making today?

   _____

   _____

   _____

   _____

   _____

_____

4. Are you living out the purpose for which God created you? What changes do you need to make so your life is in alignment with your purpose?

_____

_____

_____

_____

_____

_____

2
Cracks On The Wall

"When the storms of life come, the wicked are whirled away, but the Godly have a lasting foundation."
– Proverbs 10:25 (NLT)

One of my favorite stories that helps keep me focused on running a great race is told by Tony Evans, pastor of Oak Cliff Bible Fellowship in Dallas, TX. I first heard Dr. Evans tell this story in the Oakland Coliseum at a Promise Keepers event.

He says that one day he noticed a crack on a wall in his house. So, he called a painter over to repair the problem. The painter stripped off the old plaster, re-plastered it, and painted it. The crack was gone, the wall looked as good as new, and Mr. Evans was pleased there were no more cracks.

However, after a few weeks he noticed the crack had reappeared and this time, there were other cracks along with it. He called the painter back, frustrated that he had paid him to correct the problem, yet the problem was not fixed.

The painter apologetically redid the job and once again Mr. Evans had a new wall with no cracks.

After another couple of weeks, however, the cracks came back. Even more frustrated than before, he decided he needed a different painter – one that could actually correct the problem of the cracks on his wall.

The new painter came over, looked at the cracks on his wall and said, "I'm sorry, Mr. Evans but I cannot help you."

He said, "What do you mean you can't help me? I thought this is what you do for a living?"

The painter said, "Oh yes, this is certainly the kind of thing I do for a living, but I cannot help you because you don't have a problem with cracks on your wall."

Dr. Evans was confused and frustrated as he looked at all the cracks on his wall and said, "I'm looking at all these cracks. What do you mean I do not have a problem with cracks on my wall?"

The painter said to him, "Sir you certainly do have cracks on your wall, but that is not the problem. That is the symptom," he told him, "What you have, Mr. Evans, is a shifting foundation. As long as your foundation is shifting, you will forever have cracks on your wall. Until you solidify what's underneath, you will forever be painting over cracks on your wall."

What a powerful illustration of what we often do. We paint over the cracks in our lives, completely avoiding the real issue. Unless we solidify our foundation on Jesus Christ, we will always have cracks in our lives.

What are the cracks in your life that you have been painting over? Do you have cracks in your marriage? Cracks in your finances? In your relationships? Your character? Spiritual cracks? Emotional cracks?

Whatever the cracks are, remember they are not the problem, they are the symptom. Solidify the foundation of your life on Jesus Christ and you won't have to continually paint over the cracks in your life.

A foundational repair can be costly and inconvenient. However, the consequences of ignoring the warning signs can be disastrous. This happened in April 2013, when 1,134 people died and 2,500 people were injured after the Rana Plaza collapsed in Bangladesh.

The plaza was a five-story commercial building containing a clothing factory, a bank, apartments, and other shops. Workers saw cracks on the building walls and the bank and other shops were immediately closed. However, the factory workers were ordered to return to work the following day, in spite of the cracks. That very morning, the building collapsed, killing and injuring all those people.

What tragedy could have been avoided had they given heed to the warning signs, rather than worrying about the cost and inconvenience of closing the factory for repairs.

Whatever it takes, fix your foundation! No matter the cost or the inconvenience, make sure your foundation is built on Jesus. This foundation will hold no matter how bad things may get in your life.

Fortifying your foundation is a continual process and it starts with making time for Jesus every day. In your busy world, start the day off with Him. Give him a few moments by reading the Word, praying, and asking Him to speak to you.

Here are two of my favorite morning verses:

"Guide my steps by your word, so I will not be overcome by evil." Psalm 119:133 (NLT)

I love to read this verse and make it my prayer as I'm getting ready for my day. We build, repair, and strengthen our foundation when we ask the Lord to guide our steps according to His Word, the Bible.

Satan is real. He wants to overcome you and discourage you. He wants to get you to give up and give in. Start your day with a commitment to not allow evil to overcome you, even though it's all around you.

"Teach me your ways, O LORD, that I may live according to your truth! Grant me purity of heart, so that I may honor you." Psalm 86:11 (NLT)

This is another great verse to begin the day with. Ask God each and every morning to teach you His ways. You will not be able to live out a Godly legacy by just going to church on Sunday's and then not allowing God to work on you throughout the week. Each day, we should be learning about the truth of God's word, asking Him to give us a pure heart, and honoring Him in everything we say, think, and do.

A Foundation to Weather The Storms of Life

The storms of life are going to come. You have most likely already had some severe storms to navigate through. In fact, I have found there are three cycles of life: you're either going into a storm, you're in the middle of a storm, or you're coming out of a storm. And this cycle is continuous – that just seems to be how life is.

Jesus said in John 16:33,

"In this world you will have trouble." (NIV)

He goes on to say,

"But take heart, for I have overcome the world." (NIV)

Because Jesus overcame the world, so can you!

But how? How are you going to navigate through life's worst circumstances so that you can always overcome?

Jesus gives a great illustration of how we are going to do this in Matthew 7:24-27. Listen to what the Lord says,

"Therefore everyone who hears these words of mine and puts them into practice is like a wise man who built his house on the rock. The rain came down, the streams rose, and the winds blew and beat against that house; yet it did not fall, because it had its

foundation on the rock. But everyone who hears these words of mine and does not put them into practice is like a foolish man who built his house on sand. The rain came down, the streams rose, and the winds blew and beat against that house, and it fell with a great crash." (NIV)

The first thing we have to do is put into practice what the Lord is telling us to do. It's one thing to know what to do, it's another thing to do it. Too often we don't take action on what we know we need to do.

James 4:17 says,

"Remember, it is sin to know what you ought to do and then not do it." (NLT)

Put the words of Jesus into practice in your life and when the storms hit, your house will stand. Your marriage will stand. Your finances will stand. Your relationship with God will stand. Your character will stand. Jesus makes it clear: build your house on the Rock (on Him!) and you will stand in the fiercest of storms.

Now, this doesn't mean everything will always turn out the way we want. A relationship with Jesus doesn't mean a life with no struggles. Life brings difficulties to everyone. Having Christ as your foundation doesn't take the struggles away, it just enables you to get through the struggles and come out the other side.

You'll never be able to control what another person says or does, you may have to face consequences of past decisions, and there may be times when life is just plain unfair. But no matter what, when you build your foundation on Christ, you will get through every storm.

There's an old hymn I remember singing growing up. The words go like this:

My hope is built on nothing less than Jesus blood and righteousness. I dare not trust the sweetest frame, but wholly lean on Jesus name. On Christ the solid rock I stand, all other ground is sinking sand. All other ground is sinking sand.

Through my personal storms of going through a divorce and being separated from my kids, being let go of a coaching job, facing financial struggles, and relationship struggles, I can tell you that the solid Rock of Christ has never failed me. I've been through some tough storms, and I know there will be more storms to come. Through each storm He's made me stronger and I'm more convinced now than ever before of what my foundation must be built on.

Proverbs 10:25 says,

"When the storms of life come, the wicked are whirled away, but the Godly have a lasting foundation." (NLT)

Fighter's Stance

When I'm in the gym coaching my team, I tell them I want them in a fighter's stance. Whether you are getting ready to block out and get a rebound, help out a teammate on defense, or dive for a loose ball, you always want to look like you're ready for a fight.

A fighter's stance is one with feet shoulder width apart, knees bent, on your toes and ready to move. Having this type of foundation in sports is essential to being at your best. In contrast, a player who is standing straight up with his feet together is not ready for action and does not have the kind of foundation to perform the duties of an athlete.

Sometimes I'll illustrate this point with a player by having him stand straight up, with his feet together. I'll give him a very light push on the shoulder and the player loses his balance and nearly falls over...every time!

Then I tell him to get in the fighter's position I described above. I give him an even harder push and he stands his ground. He's solid. He's doesn't fall over.

Apply this to your own life. When you have the proper stance, you're ready for anything. This is the stance we are to take as we live out our legacy. We are to have that solid foundation we read about in Matthew 7. Our foundation must be set.

Ephesians 6:13 tells us,

"Therefore, put on every piece of God's armor so you will be able to resist the enemy in the time of evil. Then after the battle you will still be standing firm." (NLT)

The great thing is, you get to make the decision about your foundation. You and I get to decide if we will build on Christ, or on the things of this world.

What are you going to choose? Will you keep trying to repair the cracks? Or will you do the hard work of repairing the foundation?

Actions Points

1. Are there cracks in your life you have been painting over? If so, what are they and how can you repair your foundation?

   _____

   _____

   _____

   _____

2. Read Matthew 7:24-27 again. Is there anything you already know that you are not putting into practice? If so, what is it and how will you begin today?

   _____

   _____

   _____

   _____

3. Do you have a morning routine where you allot time to spend with Jesus? If not, will you begin one? What will it look like?

   _____

   _____

   _____

   _____

3
4 Keys To Building A Godly Foundation

"No one can lay any foundation other than the one already laid, which is Jesus Christ. If any man builds on this foundation using gold, silver, costly stones, wood, hay, or straw, his work will be shown for what it is, because the day will bring it to light."
— I Corinthians 3:11-13a (NIV)

In this chapter, I want to get really practical. Here's where the game plan gets down to the nitty-gritty. In order to be intentional about how you live, there are four things you must include when building a Godly foundation so that you can indeed live out the kind of legacy you want to leave.

Let's get right to it.

Key #1: Choose Christ Daily
You must be focused on building a Godly foundation every day because you will never make progress in your life on areas you don't give maximum attention to. If you are really serious about

it, it's a daily decision you make, not something you decide one day and then seldom think about again.

This is why, in chapter 10, you are going to write out your legacy statement. This will help you keep focused in the midst of a crazy work schedule, hectic family schedule, and all the other demands and temptations of life.

Jesus says in Luke 9:23,

"Whoever wants to be my disciple must deny themselves and take up their cross daily and follow me." (NIV)

Taking up your cross daily means you are committed when things are easy AND when things are difficult. When the pressure is on, you rise to the occasion. When you're with your partner and kids, when you're at work, with your friends – in all situations, you step up to the challenge of choosing Christ daily.

This is not easy. Kyle Idleman wrote a book titled, "Not a Fan: Becoming a Completely Committed Follower of Jesus". He talks about the fact that many people are fans of Jesus, but not willing to really be followers of Jesus.

Which one are you? Are you a fan of Jesus or a true follower?

Choosing to do things with your legacy in mind is often difficult when what you want at the moment is so tempting and goes against the legacy you are building. You must decide ahead of time that no matter what, you will make the right decisions.

Remember, your legacy is at stake!

28

Daily Routine

This book is all about living intentionally, so let's talk about the intentionality of your mornings. This has nothing to do with whether you're a "morning person" or not, this is about deciding how you will spend your time and making the most of it. This is about setting yourself up for success.

The most successful people in life have daily routines that guide their activities. I have studied many highly successful people, read about their lives, and listened to dozens of interviews. I have learned that success comes in all shapes and sizes, but it never comes by accident. And one thing all successful people have in common is that they are intentional about what they do from the time they get up until the time they go to bed.

Having a morning routine to help me be intentional about my day has been huge for me. My day normally starts at 4:00am and I've been getting up this early for about 4 years. In my house, that's about the only quiet time there is which allows me to focus on the things I want to get done. This book was primarily written between 4:00am and 6:00am. During this time, I also read the Bible, write out my goals, affirmations, and thanksgivings. The morning is the one part of the day I seem to have complete control over; it's time I know I can spend reading the Word and hearing from the Lord.

When do you spend your time with Jesus? Is it random, just whenever you can fit Him into your busy schedule? If so, I would imagine there are times where Jesus gets squeezed out of your day, not by design or intention, but the days just seem to work out like that.

It's time to get intentional about meeting with the Lord. Set a time that works for you. Maybe mornings are not best for you, it can be any time of day, but it's important to determine when and where you will spend your time with the Lord. We schedule and prioritize all our important meetings, so why would we not make time to purposefully schedule time with Jesus? After all, He is the most important person in all the world, right?

The quiet time you spend with the Lord is where you are strengthened and given direction and correction. You cannot build the foundation of your life if you are not regularly meeting with Him.

A solid foundation, successfully passing the baton, and living a Godly legacy all begin with choosing Christ every single day.

Key #2: Keep The Past in The Past

I Peter 5:8 tells us that Satan prowls around like a roaring lion, looking for someone to devour. He wants to destroy and discourage you and distract you from living out a great legacy. One of the ways he tries to do this is by reminding us of our past failures and sins.

Satan will do his best to keep bringing to your mind the past you are trying to forget. It's at this point we have to remember the second key to building our foundation on Christ: *Keep the past in the past.*

Always remember what God has said about your past and refuse to listen to the lies Satan tells you. The Bible tells us every single person on earth has sinned. Romans 3:23 says,

"For everyone has sinned; we all fall short of God's glorious standard." (NLT)

The Bible also tells us that we can be forgiven the moment we ask for forgiveness, and when God forgives our sins, he forgets them.

I John 1:9 says,

"If we confess our sins, he is faithful and just and will forgive us our sins and purify us from all unrighteousness." (NIV)

God is faithful. When we confess with a sincere heart, He forgives. Always. It's unconditional. When we confess our sins to Him and determine to live for Him, He always restores us to a right relationship.

In Hebrews 8:12 the Lord says,

"And I will forgive their wickedness, and I will never again remember their sins." (NLT)

And Psalm 103:12 tells us,

"He has removed our sins as far from us as the east is from the west." (NLT)

These are great promises of God that free us from the bondage of Satan's lies. And if God forgives you, you should forgive you, too. I have seen people beat themselves up over their past sins, mistakes, and failures. Don't dwell on the things God has forgiven.

Isaiah 43:19 is a great verse to cling to when we are having trouble letting go of the past. The Lord says,

"See, I am doing a new thing! Now it springs up; do you not perceive it? I am making a way in the wilderness and streams in the wasteland." (NIV)

Whenever the devil reminds you of your past, remind him of his future. God's people win and Satan and the gates of hell will go down in defeat. Your past is covered by the blood of the lamb, so you do not have to live in bondage. You are free. Free to live out your purpose and free to live out a great legacy.

God forgives, He heals, and He doesn't want you living discouraged or defeated. He wants you to live in victory because you are forgiven. There will be others who do not forgive you, but remember, God always forgives.

There may be ramifications of our actions and difficulties because of the choices we have made. But don't ever forget that God has a plan for you to live life to the absolute fullest, in spite of your past. This means we must move beyond it.

When I'm coaching, I tell my players I don't ever expect them to play a perfect game, but I do expect them to learn from their mistakes. Athletes at even the highest level make mistakes and do things they wish they could take back. That's just the nature of sports and of being human.

The key is knowing what you do when a mistake happens. Do you stop and have a pity party? Or do you accept responsibility and move on?

Accept responsibility, learn from your mistakes, and move forward. I'm always telling my team there are three things you should always do with a mistake:

1. Admit it
2. Learn from it
3. Forget it

I've known people over the years who have a difficult time admitting to their mistakes. They don't want to accept responsibility and instead, point the finger elsewhere. Do you know anyone like that? Let's make sure that person is not us!

Once you are able to accept personal responsibility, then, and only then, are you able to learn from it. There is always a lesson to learn in every situation. Someone once said, "There's winning and there's learning." You choose if you will learn from your mistakes.

Forgetting your mistakes is a decision you make to stop letting the guilt and disappointment hold you back. You won't literally forget your mistakes, but in order to move forward, you cannot continue to dwell on them. It's over. It's in the past. It's time to move forward.

Remember, Christ forgives and doesn't hold it against you any longer. Romans 8:1 tells us,

"So now there is no condemnation for those who belong to

Christ Jesus." (NLT)

Let go of the past and live out the incredible future that God has in store for you. This is your destiny. This is your legacy.

Key #3: Get Around Godly People

I cannot overemphasize the importance of this third key. If you really want to have a solid foundation on Christ, then key #3 must be a major part of your life: Get around Godly people. Being around other people who have the same desires as you will help you be the kind of person you really want to be.

Having a Godly foundation means your mind is focused on the right things. When you are around others who are like-minded, it helps you keep focused on the right things. When you are around those who are not like-minded, you will find yourself battling to keep your thoughts and priorities in check.

Jim Rhon once said that you are the average of the five people you associate with most and I have found this to be true. John Maxwell says, "You can't soar with the eagles if you're hanging out with the turkeys."

If you are a student and you want to get good grades, you should hang out with other students who get good grades. When you do this, you will start to do what they do, think how they think, and have the same attitudes towards working on your studies they do. If you want to get good grades but you're always hanging around kids who get D's and F's, you will have conversations, thoughts, and attitudes that lead towards low grades. Before long, you will find yourself with grades way lower than your potential.

If you want to lose weight and get in shape, you should hang around those who have already done it, or are successfully doing it. You will then start to think about food and exercise in the same way they do. Their habits will more easily become your habits and your conversations will be about achieving the common goal you share. You will have their support and encouragement and they will have yours. Your like-mindedness will give you a feeling of power and accomplishment and create momentum.

If you want to live out a Godly legacy, get around other men and women who also want to live out a Godly legacy. In doing this, you will have conversations that strengthen you and enable you to live the way you want to live. Your like-mindedness will help you live your life for Christ and strengthen your foundation like never before.

It's a powerful thing to know there are other people who have the same struggles you have, the same desires you have, the same goals you have, and the same desire for Christ that you have.

When I speak at youth events about this subject, I often tell them what Rick Warren says, "Your friends are the number one factor that will determine whether you succeed or fail in life."

That's a big statement, but I believe it. I think the reason this is so true is rooted in these three powerful verses about our friends and associations:

I Corinthians 15:33 says,

"Do not be misled: Bad company corrupts good character." (NIV)

I love that this verse tells us "not to be misled'. When I was growing up, my dad was very picky about who he allowed me to hang out with. It made me so frustrated sometimes, but he knew what he was doing. He wasn't about to take the chance of allowing someone to corrupt my character when he was working so hard to build me up in Christ.

I see young people (and adults, too) who have friends they know they need to disconnect with but don't. They get sucked into believing they will have a positive influence on them, when that seldom, if ever, happens. As parents, we must carefully monitor who we allow our children to hang out with. And as men and women of God, we must also closely monitor who we hang out with ourselves.

Very seldom does it work from the top down. When it's a one-to-one ratio, it almost always works from the bottom up. Meaning negative character will have more of an influence on positive character than positive character will have on negative. When my friend Chris Johnson was a youth director, he would illustrate this point by having one person stand on a chair and ask that person to pull the person next to them up onto the chair with them. Then he would ask the person standing next to the chair to pull the other person off the chair. Which one do you think had the easier task?

Proverbs 27:17 says,

"As iron sharpens iron, so one person sharpens another." (NIV)

Who is sharpening you? Who in your life helps to motivate and encourage you to live out a Godly legacy? Who do you have conversations with about the things of God? About handling temptations? About being the person that God has called you to be?

Proverbs 13:20 sums it all up with this,

"Walk with the wise and become wise, for a companion of fools suffers harm." (NIV)

Right now, take a moment and evaluate who you are spending your time with. If you are the average of the five people you hang out with most, what is your average? Your legacy will never be greater than this average.

Virtual Influencers

With the technology available to us today, you can ensure you are being influenced by the right people. Through videos, podcasts, webinars, blogs, and social media you can choose almost anyone in the world to learn from. And you can spend time with them!

I first learned this almost 25 years ago, long before the technology we have now. When I was in my early 20's, my pastor, Mark Bernhardt, introduced me to a monthly cassette tape club called "Injoy Life Club" by John Maxwell. At the time, John was the pastor of Skyline Wesleyan Church in San Diego, CA, and sent out a monthly cassette tape on leadership. Mark had an entire library of tapes and gave me access to all of them. I listened to every one of them and soaked up the content. Many of my leadership ideas and principles were established during this time when I immersed myself in the content.

Around the same time, I learned of Tony Robbins and fell in love with his "Awaken the Giant" and "Unleash" programs. I listened over and over again and filled up notebooks with notes that I still have to this day.

I spent about 18 months soaking up hours and hours of knowledge and wisdom from these two men. I've never met either one of them, but they have made available the essence of who they are and what they know for anyone to grab ahold of. This period of my life was the most significant growth period I've ever had.

Today, there is so much amazing content available online, both free and paid. I have learned from some amazing people such as Tony Evans, Steven Furtick, Michael Hyatt, Lewis Howes, Dale Carnegie, Grant Baldwin, Eric Thomas, and Craig Groeschel, just to name a few. It seems a week doesn't go by when I learn of someone new who has been where I want to be and done what I want to do. Whether it's a book, podcast, webinar, video, social media channel, or a paid program, it's so important to invest your time with others you can learn from.

There are times when I haven't been around enough "eagles" and I feel myself starting to drift from my purpose, or start feeling like I'm the only one who thinks the way I do. If I'm not able to physically be in the presence of those who lift me up, I will often listen to a podcast or watch a video of one of my virtual mentors who I know will lift my spirits.

You get to decide who you spend the most time with. And that decision will make all the difference in the world.

Key #4: It's a Slow Process

Anything worthwhile in life will take time and will not be easy. I see people all the time who are frustrated by their lack of progress, whether it's spiritually, financially, physically, or perhaps relationally with a family member or close friend.

Somehow, we get this idea in our heads that we can get where we want to go overnight. This is not true in any area of life, especially when it comes to our spiritual development.

Do you know someone in your life who is much older than you that just seems to have all the wisdom in the world? They did not get that way overnight. As you build the foundation of your life on Jesus Christ, remember, it's not a project you can do in a day. It's a lifetime of building.

Slow progress is still progress. Don't get discouraged, just remember it takes time.

I have the Nike app on my phone and use it to track the miles I run. As of writing this, I have logged 843.2 miles. When I look at that I'm amazed to think that I am closing in on running 1000 miles. Are you impressed? You might be really impressed if I told you I did that in just a couple of months.

The truth is, it's taken me about 5 years to get to this point. I'm not an avid runner; I run 2-3 times a week and only a mile or two at a time. Though it sounds impressive that I've logged close to 1000 miles, it's taken me a very long time to get there!

The same is true with our spiritual growth. It's your consistency that counts more than anything – your consistency is key for living out a great legacy. Consistency will take you a very long way; it just won't take you there fast. But remember, fast is not the goal, finishing is!

Paul tells us in Philippians 1:6 what he is certain of. He says,

"I am certain that God, who began a good work within you, will continue his work until it is finally finished on the day when Christ Jesus returns." (NLT)

God is faithful. There was a time He began a great work in you and He wants to continue His work. It's a process that will go on your entire life...until the day when Jesus comes back to take us home to be with Him.

When you are feeling discouraged, when you are feeling like you're not making progress, when you feel like you are just not where you want to be, remember almighty God who began that good work in you will continue that work. You just have to let Him. Don't give up.

I Quit!

Whenever I'm feeling discouraged and I want to give up, I think of an old poster I once saw. It was put out by the Fellowship of Christian Athletes and it was a picture of a football player sitting on a bench, dejected. His helmet was on the ground, his head was in his hands; it was the picture of complete defeat. The caption across the top read in big letters, "I Quit!"

At first look it wasn't a very inspiring picture. In fact, unless you looked closely at the poster, you wondered what the point of it was. Was it letting us know that when the going gets really tough, sometimes we just have to give up? No! When the going gets extremely difficult, we think of our savior. In the bottom corner of the poster was a small picture of an old, rugged cross and right next to it were the words, "He didn't."

Jesus went through the ultimate challenge and difficulty. The truth is, most people have no idea how hard it was for Him to go through the torture of the cross. Certainly, those of us who live in America, with all our freedoms and comforts cannot really fathom what He did. But He did it for you and for me. He went to that cross, He endured pain and suffering, and He did not quit.

Neither can you. You can't quit! Keep going because the fire you are going through is only making you become more like Him. The fire doesn't define you, it refines you.

Calico was a town in California built in the 1880s. Today, this ghost town out in the desert of Southern California has become a popular tourist attraction. A few years ago, a fire destroyed some of the original structures that were made out of wood. But the solid brick that was used was not burned – it survived the fire.

If you're made of the right stuff, you can survive the fire you are going through. Every day, God is molding you, shaping you, and helping you to become more like Him. In the most difficult parts of your life, you must have a foundation that will hold you and sustain you. If you make Jesus Christ that foundation, you will come out better than you were before.

As we close out this part of the book about building a foundation, look to what I Corinthians 3:11-15 says,

"No one can lay any foundation other than the one already laid, which is Jesus Christ. If any man builds on this foundation using gold, silver, costly stones, wood, hay, or straw, his work will be shown for what it is, because the day will bring it to light. It will be revealed with fire, and the fire will test the quality of each person's work. If what has been built survives, the builder will receive a reward. If it is burned up, the builder will suffer loss..." (NIV)

Action Points

Before we move on to Part 2, take a moment to contemplate the four keys to building a Godly foundation and then go through the eight action points.

1. Describe your relationship with Jesus. Are you more of a fan or follower?

   _____

   _____

   _____

   _____

   _____

   _____

2. Do you have a morning routine? If not, write out a schedule for your morning for at least the first 90 minutes of your day.

   _____

   _____

   _____

   _____

   _____

   _____

3. What is in your past that you need to let go of?

   _____

   _____

_____

_____

_____

_____

4. How well do you understand that it's a long process to become the person God wants you to be?

_____

_____

_____

_____

_____

5. What can you do to keep yourself focused on the Lord and not get discouraged when things get difficult?

_____

_____

_____

_____

_____

6. If you are the average of the five people you are around most, on a scale of 1 to 10, what is your average right now?

_____

7. Who are the key people in your life that are shaping you? Are there any people you need to start spending less time with?

_____

_____

_____

_____

_____

_____

8. Do you have any virtual mentors you can learn from? Who are they?

_____

_____

_____

_____

_____

_____

PART 2
Feed Your Faith

4

It's Always An Inside Job!

"The LORD does not look at the things people look at. People look at the outward appearance, but the LORD looks at the heart."
– I Samuel 16:7 (NLT)

"Be more concerned with your character than your reputation. Your character is what you really are while your reputation is merely what others think you are."
– John Wooden

I want you to do an exercise. Think of someone you really admire; someone who is living the kind of legacy that really stands out to you. Now, grab a pen and paper and write down their name. Next, I want you to take a minute and think about why you admire this person and write down all the qualities they have that cause you to think so highly of them.

As you look at the list of qualities, chances are 90% of what you wrote down has more to do with attitude traits than skill or talent. This is a good exercise because it shows us the qualities we admire most in people usually have more to do with attitudes than anything else.

Attitude is a decision. The character traits you have are the result of the decisions you make. We don't always control what we are naturally good at in terms of talent or skill, but we can always control our attitude.

The legacy you are going to leave begins on the inside. What people see on the outside is simply a result of what's going on inside. You must make a decision to live from the inside out because what's on the inside will always show up on the outside.

Jesus made this point when he told the Pharisees in Matthew 23 that they were blind to how this all works. He told them in verse 26,

"First wash the inside of the cup and the dish, and then the outside will become clean, too." (NLT)

They, like many of us, were too concerned with the outside. But Jesus wants our top priority to be the inside. He says first things first – deal with the inside (your character, your heart, your motives) and the outside (what people see) will take care of itself.

I constantly hear people talk about wanting great success. There's nothing wrong with this and we all have something inside of us that wants to do well in life. But whether it's your career, your finances, your ministry, your family, or any other area of life, here is a truth we all need to understand:

Before you can *have* you must *do*, and before you can do you

must *be.*

Everything starts with who you are on the inside. Before you can have great success, you must do the things that lead to success; but before you can do those things, you have to be the kind of person that is able to do those things. You can't skip steps. Let me say it again:

Before you can have you must do, and before you can do, you must be.

My Story - Something More

I have been a teacher and coach since I graduated from college in 1991. I've always loved working with young people, both in the classroom and on the basketball court. I've been living in Stockton, CA for 13 years and I love the roots I have put down in my community and the small platform being a teacher and coach has given me to share my faith and positive messages.

About five or six years ago, I began to sense God stirring something inside of me. I felt He was saying, "Gary, I have more in store for you." It was clear to me that God was talking, but at the time I wasn't sure what He was talking about. I didn't know exactly what direction God was leading me, and what my next actions should be. I remember being confused and frustrated.

Have you ever been there?

I could have tried to ignore it. After all, I've taught and coached for over two decades; most teachers at this stage of their careers are realizing they are closer to the end than the beginning. A part of me wanted to keep doing what I was doing and just be content with where I was. I was in my comfort zone and I liked being there. But I couldn't ignore what was going on inside of me, and I couldn't get away from this stirring that God was telling me He had more in store for me. I knew staying in my comfort zone was not an option.

As time has gone by, God has given me more direction for my ministry and influence. Slowly but faithfully at His pace, not mine. Little by little I see God using me in ways that He wasn't using me just a few years ago. For the longest time, God didn't tell me specifically what He wanted me to do. Looking back on it, I think God knew before He could take me to the next level in my life, my ministry, and my influence, He had to work on me from the inside out. He wasn't ready to have me *do* more, because He first wanted me to *be* more. The "being" was the preparation I needed before the "doing" could take place.

Maybe you have a similar stirring inside of you. I believe that one of the reasons I wrote this book was to help someone respond to the voice of God calling them to more; more influence and more impact on others. Perhaps you are right where I was, hung up on the doing or the having.

Has your prayer been, "God what do you want me to do?" If that's been your prayer and you're not getting direction, then change your prayer to, "God what do you want me to *be*?" When you focus on being the person God is calling you to be, the doing and the having will eventually follow.

The key is to constantly pray this prayer, "God, lead me and I will follow, whatever it is." For me, I had two or three different things

I felt God might be calling me towards. I wrestled for a long time about possibly becoming a full-time pastor or going back to coaching at the collegiate level. I also always had a desire to motivate and speak to people and wondered if God was calling me to full-time public speaking.

I just kept praying and kept following open doors. I'm still doing that today and don't ever plan to stop! God is continually opening and closing doors in my life and my job is to simply go through the doors He opens up.

I have spent 28 years as a basketball coach and math teacher. Currently, I am still teaching in a public school but at the same time focusing on helping as many people as possible with the message of living intentionally. God has given me opportunities to speak to churches and church groups. He has also opened doors for me to speak to businesses and organizations. A part of my journey was nine months as an interim pastor, getting the opportunity to preach every Sunday. I don't know where I will be in 5, 10 or 20 years, but I know that I will never stop humbly praying, "God, lead me and I will follow...whatever it is!"

What is your story?

God created you on purpose, for a purpose. As you develop your game plan for leaving a Godly legacy, remember God wants to use you in incredible ways. Unfortunately, He doesn't always reveal the details all at once. This is because He wants you to trust Him. He wants to know you have complete faith in Him. He wants you to focus on *being* before *doing*. It's not by your own strength, your own wisdom, or your own power; everything you have and every opportunity that comes your way is from God.

Sowing Legacy Seeds

Paul gives us a powerful truth in 2 Corinthians 9:6. He says,

"Whoever sows sparingly will also reap sparingly, and whoever sows generously will also reap generously." (NIV)

This is a principle most people learned when they were young. I can still hear my mom saying, "Gary, you reap what you sow!"

When it comes to your legacy, I want you to think about this powerful verse. Right now, today, you are sowing seeds. Where you will be tomorrow will be a result of the seeds you are sowing today. And where you are today is a result of the seeds you sowed in the past.

Too many people, especially those nearing mid-life, don't understand this. It's not your circumstances, or chance, or blind luck that has put you where you are today. It's not the things you've had no control over, either. You are where you are and you are what you are because of the seeds you have sown. In other words, it's the choices you have made in spite of your circumstances that have brought you to where you are today.

Now, I understand it's quite possible that some terrible things, completely beyond your control, may have happened to you. I think of Amy Purdy, an avid snowboarder, who at age 19 contracted bacterial meningitis. She ended up having both of her legs amputated just below the knees. She lost both of her kidneys and her spleen had to be removed. A tragedy to this beautiful, athletic 19-year-old who was full of life.

You can imagine how devasting this must have been. Many people would have given up on life after an experience like this. They would have gone for years, perhaps their whole life defeated and in despair.

Not Amy.

If you look at her Instagram page, you will see nothing but smiles and positivity. On the about page on her website (amypurdy.com) the first line says, "Amy has lived an incredible life". I have never met Amy but I heard her story and have followed her for some time. There are few people in the world who have a better outlook on life than her. She is back on her snowboard, and in 2014, she won the bronze at the Sochi Paralympics.

I also think of Elizabeth Smart who was abducted from her home in Salt Lake City, Utah on June 5, 2002. She was held captive for nine months by Brian Mitchell and Wanda Barzee. She was tied up, raped daily, and threatened with death if she tried to escape. On March 12, 2003, she managed to escape from the house she was in and get to the street where a police officer rescued her.

The physical, mental, and emotional wounds that she endured are mind-boggling. I can't even fathom it. Yet, Elizabeth now travels around the country speaking as a child safety activist and is a contributor to ABC news. She has written two books, the last one titled, "Where There is Hope".

I don't know what has happened to you in your past or what you may currently be going through. I pray it hasn't been anything as tragic as these two examples I've given here. But I want you to know that you do not have to be a victim any longer. God has given you the victory to overcome whatever is in your past that you had no control over.

But thanks be to God! He gives us the victory through our Lord Jesus Christ. I Corinthians 15:57 (NIV)

Your Godly legacy is not dependent on the situation you have been in. The tragic things you have gone through shape you but do not have to define you. You are defined by the blood of Jesus who loves you and gave His life for you.

The good news is, no matter what your past, you can choose today to sow the right kind of seeds; you can start sowing legacy seeds right now. One day when you and I are gone, our legacy will be the result of the seeds we have sown during our lifetime. Sow your legacy seeds in spite of whatever circumstances you find yourself in.

As John Maxwell says, "You cannot go back and create a new beginning, but you can start now and create a new ending."

Two Principles of Sowing Seeds

There are two principles of sowing I want you to think about.

The first principle: The return is always greater than the one seed that was sown.

Not only will you reap what you sow, but you will reap more than what you sow. My daughter, Grace, loves to help me in our garden. We carefully plant a green bean or corn seed in the ground. But when we sow one corn seed, we don't get one corn seed back, we get hundreds! We plant one green bean seed and we don't just get back one, but we get many.

When you sow the right kind of seeds, they have a multiplication effect. They don't just impact those who are immediately close to you, but the people you've impacted will now be able to positively impact others.

Your legacy seeds will yield a great return!

The second principle: There is always a delay.

If you plant a garden like Grace and I do, then you know you don't plant seeds on a Saturday afternoon and go out on Sunday to reap a harvest. That would be nice, but that's not how it works when you sow seeds; whether it's green beans or your legacy!

The impact of your life is not always immediately known. But over time, with proper watering and nurturing, your legacy seeds will yield a crop beyond what you ever thought was possible.

Many of us are familiar with the writings of American author, Henry David Thoreau. Thoreau is well known for his work, but it wasn't until after he died that his fame really began to spread. Thoreau worked in a pencil factory and occasionally published an article but it wasn't until several years after he died that Henry Stephens Salt wrote a biography of Thoreau, earning him great posthumous fame.[1]

---

[1] mmn.com by Melissa Bryeer, (June 18, 2013)

Another example is Johann Sebastian Bach. His name is a very familiar name around the globe, but it wasn't until 1829 (almost 80 years after his death), when German composer Felix Mendelssohn reintroduced Bach's "Passion According to St. Matthew", that Bach began to be known as the great composer he was.[2]

There is always a delay when you sow seeds, but if you sow them right, the harvest will come.

You and I will never fully know the impact and reach of our lives. But one day when you stand before the Father in Heaven, you will see the results. So, for now, you have to keep living the right way. You have to keep sowing those legacy seeds and make a decision every day that you will live out that legacy you want to leave; even when you think no one even notices.

Remember this verse from Galatians when you feel like you're not seeing the results you want:

So let's not get tired of doing what is good. At just the right time we will reap a harvest of blessing if we don't give up. Galatians 6:9 (NLT)

In the next two chapters, we are going to talk about how faith is essential to sowing our legacy seeds.

---

[2] mmn.com by Melissa Bryeer (June 18, 2013)

Action Points

1. Are you more concerned with the inside than the outside? Describe some inside character traits you need to work on to become more like Jesus.

   _____

   _____

   _____

   _____

2. Are you content with where you are in life? If God is calling you to something more, are you more concerned with "doing" and "having" or are you more concerned with "being" the person He wants you to be?

   _____

   _____

   _____

   _____

3. What are some legacy seeds you are currently sowing that will result in a harvest later on?

   _____

   _____

   _____

   _____

5
What Is Faith?

"And it is impossible to please God without faith..."
– Hebrews 11: 6 (NLT)

"Faith grows when it is planted in the fertile soil of God's word."
– Billy Graham

"Faith is taking the first step even when you don't see the whole staircase."
– Martin Luther King

To effectively sow seeds that will bring about a Godly legacy, you must have faith.

Hebrews 11:6 says,

"And it is impossible to please God without faith. Anyone who wants to come to him must believe that God exists and that he rewards those who sincerely seek him." (NLT)

Faith can be a tricky thing. I think the word "faith" gets thrown around a lot and is used a bit too casually. You hear people talk about "blind faith" or he took a "leap of faith" or he is a "person of faith" or that is a "faith-based organization".

These are common terms and I've used them myself, but what do those phrases really mean? I'm not sure they accurately paint a picture of someone who has completely placed their faith and trust in Jesus Christ. And that is at the heart of real faith.

Charles Blondin was a tight rope walker. Many years ago, he would dazzle crowds with his ability to walk without a safety net across a tight rope in very dangerous situations.

The story is told of when he strung a tight rope across Niagara Falls. With crowds on both sides, he carefully walked on this tight rope across the falls and back again. Each time he made it across, the crowds would cheer and applaud, going crazy at this feat. He was so good that he would walk across the tight rope carrying objects from one side of the falls to the other, including pushing a wheelbarrow.

After going across pushing the wheelbarrow, the crowd continuing their cheers, he asked them if they believed he could push a wheelbarrow across the falls with a person inside? The crowd screamed with excitement and yelled an emphatic yes! They all wanted to see this!

Charles said, "Great! Who will be my volunteer?"

All of a sudden, the crowd got very quiet as no one wanted to volunteer. They all said they thought he could do it, but when push came to shove, they weren't so sure and no one wanted to get in.

I think a lot of Christians are like this. We cheer God on and sing about how great He is on Sunday's at church. We have our times of worship and tell God we have faith in Him. But at the same time we refuse to get in the wheelbarrow. When it comes right down to it, we don't really do what God is telling us to do. We're content to cheer Him and praise Him and tell Him how great He is, but when it comes to really demonstrating our faith in Him, we back away.

When Jesus met Peter walking on the water, Peter began to sink because he took his eyes off Jesus. Jesus reached out, saved him and said, "Oh you of little faith. Why do you doubt?"

Sometimes I feel God looks at me and says, "Oh Gary, you have so little faith. Why do you doubt?"

We must keep our eyes fixed on Jesus. We must also remember that Jesus said in Luke 17:6,

"If you had faith even as small as a mustard seed, you could say to this mulberry tree, 'May you be uprooted and thrown into the sea,' and it would obey you!'" (NLT)

I want my faith to grow and, over time, I know it will. However, you don't have to start off with great faith, you only need to act on the faith you have. Each time you do this, it will grow a little more. Your faith will become a little stronger each time you use the faith you have.

Defining Faith

What exactly is faith? We know we need it, but let's see if we can define it and apply it to our lives to help us define our legacy. Hebrews describes it as,

"Faith is the confidence that what we hope for will actually happen; it gives us assurance about things we cannot see." Hebrews 11:1 (NLT)

I personally love how Tony Evans puts it. He says, "Faith is acting like God is telling the truth." He goes on to say, faith is "acting like it is so, even when it isn't so, in order that it might be so, simply because God said so."

You got that? That's what faith is!

Living out a great legacy means that when people look at your life they see faith in action. They see a person who lives every day as if all of God's promises are true, even when it seems like they're not. Do you have complete confidence in God to believe that He will do exactly what He says?

The Faith Test

The real test of your faith is when things are not going well. When things seem to be falling apart, do you continue to cling to Jesus? Is it evident to those around you? A legacy-minded person is calm and cool under pressure because they know the One who will keep them and protect them and see them through.

Anyone can have faith when things are good. That's easy to do.

But can you still exercise your faith in God when things are not going according to plan?

I love the song by Mercy Me, "Even If". Part of the lyrics go like this:

> I know You're able and I know You can
> Save through the fire with Your mighty hand.
> But even if You don't
> My hope is in You alone
> They say it only takes a little faith
> To move a mountain,
> Well good thing
> A little faith is all I have, right now.
> But God, when You choose
> To leave mountains unmovable
> Oh give me the strength to be able to sing
> It is well with my soul.
> You've been faithful, You've been good
> All of my days
> Jesus, I will cling to You
> Come what may

The big question you need to ask yourself is, are you going to cling to Jesus even when you are going through the fire? That's the kind of faith that leaves a legacy.

You Don't Always Have to Feel Faith
We are emotional beings. We feel emotions every day and some of us struggle to keep our emotions in check. Even though God made us this way, our faith and our emotions do not go together.

You can live in faith even when you don't feel faith. This is important for us to understand.

Your ability to live in faith and by faith is independent of you feeling faith. There will be times you just don't feel it. That's ok. You can still act in faith anyway. Faith is not measured by the way we *feel*, but by the way we *act*.

Can you still act in faith even when you are not feeling it? Can you make decisions in your life, both big and small, based on your faith in Christ, no matter what feeling or emotion you are having?

Faith is not a feeling, it is a decision.

To live out a great legacy, we must make a decision every day to feed our faith. When we feed it, it grows; it becomes stronger. If you don't feed it, it becomes weaker. What you feed in your life will grow, and what you starve will die, so we must feed our faith and starve everything that is contrary to the things of God.

Story of Two Dogs
One of my favorite tales illustrates this point so well. There was an old Inuit fisherman who owned two dogs. One was a black dog, the other was white. He trained these two dogs to fight on command. On Saturday's, he'd take his two dogs to the town square to fight and he would take bets on which dog would win.

Some weeks the black dog would win, other weeks the white dog would win, but the fisherman always won. Somehow, he seemed to always know which dog would win the fight. Week after week this went on, with the fisherman always knowing which dog would win.

Finally, his friends asked, "Every week you know which dog will win. How in the world do you always know?"

The old fisherman chuckled and said, "It's pretty easy really. You see, the week before I feed one dog and starve the other. The dog I feed is stronger so it wins the fight."

This old tale illustrates that inside of you and I are two dogs. You could say one is a good dog, represented by the Lord and all the Godly things you want your life to stand for. The other dog is selfish, self-centered, and wants the things of the world more than the things of God. Whichever one you feed is going to win.

There is always a battle going on inside between good and evil...between what you want and what God wants...the good dog and the bad dog.

Please hear this well as I repeat this statement: *Whichever one you feed is going to win!*

When you become a Christian, the bad dog doesn't automatically go away. In fact, it begins to fight even more so it's all the more important that you starve that dog and feed the other one.

The Bible talks about sanctification and the battle for control after we accept Christ into our heart. Who is going to call the shots in your life? In my personal experience, even after committing my entire life to the Lord and His purposes, that decision doesn't completely take away my human desires that are contrary to God.

Over time, my desires have become more Godly and more in line with His will, BUT it's only because I constantly try to feed that part of my life.

This goes back to the importance of choosing Christ daily. It's a daily decision to feed on the things of God and starve the things of the world.

There will always be a battle when you choose to feed your faith, but remember, if you keep on the right path you are going to be victorious. After all, Romans 8:37 says,

"...despite all these things, overwhelming victory is ours through Christ, who loved us." (NLT)

That doesn't mean you're just barely going to get the win on a last-second shot. No! This means a landslide victory is yours if you keep feeding your faith on a daily basis.

Action Points

1. Are you the kind of person who needs to be "certain"? Describe your faith and how willing you'd be to get in the wheelbarrow.

   _____

   _____

   _____

   _____

2. Do you tend to have more faith when things are going well? Describe a time when you exercised faith in a difficult situation.

   _____

   _____

   _____

   _____

3. Are you feeding your faith and starving the things of the world? What can you do to feed your faith even more?

   _____

   _____

   _____

   _____

6

The Opposite Of Faith

"For we walk by faith, not by sight."
– I Corinthians 5:7 (NLT)

"If you can dream it you can achieve it. Remember, this whole thing started with a mouse."
– Walt Disney

What do you believe is the opposite of faith? When I speak on this subject I always ask this question and the two most common answers I get are always "doubt" and "fear". However, I don't think this is accurate. I believe doubt and fear and barriers to faith, not the opposite of faith.

If we are going to really live in faith and feed our faith, it is important that we understand the other side of the coin.

I first heard Steven Furtick use this word to describe the opposite of faith: *certainty.*

I agree with this. The opposite of faith is being certain. Think about it. If you are certain about something, then there is no need for faith. Exercising faith requires a sense of not knowing; that's why we have faith.

I have to admit, this is really hard for me. I'm the kind of guy who needs to know. I need to have a plan, I need to know the plan, and I need to be CERTAIN about it. The positive side of this quality is that it helps me be intentional. The negative side of this, however, is that I have a hard time trusting and living in faith when I don't know.

I do believe God wants us to plan and He expects us to prepare for things to the best of our ability. But to really live in faith is to move forward even when you are not certain of the outcome or the process. If you know God is calling you to something, you don't have to have all the details figured out. You don't have to have every question answered. There will be times when God wants you to move even though you have a lot of uncertainty.

If you act only when you are certain, then you are not living in faith. And remember Hebrews 11:6 tells us that without faith, we cannot please God. If you know God wants you to move, don't wait until you have it all figured out. That's not your job. God's job is to figure it all out, which He has already done. Don't think that just because he hasn't told you, He doesn't know. He *does* know. Your job is to simply obey.

Is there any area in your life where God is talking to you about moving forward but you're reluctant? Are you waiting to get more information? Are you waiting until you get more answers? Are you waiting until you are "more sure"? I'm not devaluing waiting time. That is important and is the subject of another whole book! But perhaps you're at a point right now where God has brought you and now He's just waiting on you to make a move.

Walk by Faith, Not by Sight

The African Impala is an incredible animal. It can jump to a height of 10-20 feet and cover a distance of 30 feet. There are few creatures like it. But did you know the Africa Impala can be kept in a zoo by a wall that's only 3 feet high? It could easily jump over the wall and clear it by several feet, but it doesn't because the African Impala will not jump where it cannot see. If it cannot see where it's going to land, it won't jump.

Faith in God is jumping when He says jump, even though you cannot see where you are going to land. Too many people are living well below their God-given potential, locked up like an animal in the zoo. Even though they have the power and the ability to be free, they refuse to jump because they don't have faith.

2 Corinthians 5:7 says,

"For we walk by faith, not by sight." (ESV)

As Christians striving to live out a Godly legacy, we must make a decision every day to live by faith and not by sight.

I'll See It When I Believe It

You've heard the saying before, "I'll believe it when I see it." When it comes to living our lives in faith, this isn't how the Christian is supposed to live.

Instead, we need to turn that around and say, "I'll see it when I believe it."

When you live in faith, you see it your own mind first, before it ever becomes a reality. You see it, you taste it, you smell it, you live it in your mind's eye first. This principle is so important for every area of your life.

If you are going to accomplish something significant for God, you have to believe it's possible. You have to see it in your mind and believe in your heart that through God's power it's possible. When you really believe that God is able to do exceedingly, abundantly more than you could ever imagine, then you will begin to see it become a reality.

But you must believe it first!

You Choose What You Want to Believe

Rick Warren tells the story that in the 1960s, the Russians sent their first cosmonaut into outer space. He circled the earth and when he came back down, he held a press conference and said, "I searched the heavens, and I looked for God, and I did not see him anywhere. Therefore, there is no God."

The communists, which was an atheistic regime, said, "We now have scientific proof that there is no God."

About six months later, John Glenn went into outer space, circled the earth three times on Gemini, came back down, held a press conference and said, "I saw God everywhere! I saw his glory in the galaxy. I saw His splendor in the universe. I saw His Majesty in the stars."

Who was right? They both were. Scripture tells us that people will believe what their itching ears want to believe. 2 Timothy 4:3 says,

"For a time is coming when people will no longer listen to sound and wholesome teaching. They will follow their own desires and will look for teachers who will tell them whatever their itching ears want to hear." (NLT)

As with everything in life, it really comes down to a choice; what are you going to believe?

When you don't have all the answers, you must make a choice to live by faith and to feed your faith every day.

Fear and Doubt

As I mentioned at the beginning of this chapter, fear and doubt are huge barriers to faith. Fear is paralyzing. When you give in to fear, it will always hold you back and keep you from living out the legacy you are trying to leave.

I Timothy 1:7 gives us this great truth,

"For God has not given us a spirit of fear and timidity, but of power, love, and self-discipline." (NLT)

You are meant to live with God's power at work in your life, fueled by faith. Living with God's power rather than fear does not mean you never experience fear. I believe in many situations there will always be a presence of fear; I'm not sure you can ever get rid of it altogether. However, every time you feel fear, courage is always present as well.

It's simply a matter of which you will choose. You can choose to allow fear to dominate your thinking or you can choose to let courage take charge.

I love the acronyms for what we choose to do with fear:

Face Everything And Rise

...Or...

Forget Everything And Run

The choice is yours. You choose how to respond to the fears you have. Perhaps you've run in the past, refusing to face it and rise. Today is a new day. You can decide that you will no longer run from your fears, but face them head on.

This acronym will help you remember what fear really is. Fear is simply:

False Evidence Appearing Real

Usually the things we fear don't ever come to pass. As Franklin Roosevelt said, "We have nothing to fear but fear itself."

What are you fearing in your life? Are you allowing fear and doubt to hold you back and keep you from being all that God has called you to be? Your legacy is dependent on you stepping out in faith, so have the courage to move forward in spite of fear.

Fearless Faith

I love the idea of "fearless faith".

Take that word "fearless" and think about what it means. What people come to mind when you think of someone who is fearless? I think of athletes I've coached that play fearlessly. That is, they give everything they've got without regard for the consequences. They are the kind of players that will run through a brick wall if that's what the coach asks of them. They don't ask why, they don't think twice, they just do what needs to be done for their team to win.

That's a fearless athlete!

On a much larger scale, when I think of the word fearless, I think of Navy Seal Adam Brown, a Christian who helped capture Osama Bin Laden but lost his life in the process.

I think of Martin Luther King's "I have a dream speech" or the "Tank Man" in Tiananmen Square in the late 1990s.

Take your idea of what fearless means and put it together with the word "faith". Now we're talking about someone doing great things for the Lord. A Christian living in fearless faith is one who is bold, courageous, and gives no regard for consequences, but does the right thing regardless; a true warrior for the Lord.

Can you see it? That's the kind of legacy you were created to live!

When you are a fearless faith Christian, you understand that all things are possible, that one person can make a significant difference by daring to stand out, daring to live audaciously for the Lord.

Almost

Too many people live an almost life. One of the saddest words in the English language is "almost". People set goals and *almost* reach them; they go on diets and *almost* lose all the weight; they have relationships that *almost* work out. I see men and women in our churches today who are *almost* what God has called them to be.

In Acts 26, the Apostle Paul was brought to trial before King Agrippa. He took the opportunity to give his testimony about Jesus and share his faith. He laid it all out there and told the King everything about who Jesus is and what He had done. When he finished, he said some words that I am sure are haunting him 2,000 years later. He said to Paul,

"Almost you persuade me to be a Christian." Acts 26:28 (AKJV)

Almost. He was so close. But almost won't get him into heaven and almost won't leave the legacy you want to leave.

Many give up before they get there. What about you? When it comes to living life the way God intended, don't stop short. Don't be someone who almost receives God's blessings, and almost lives out their legacy. Pursue fearless faith in God. Live large in Christ. Say yes to Him in every way and believe that He is indeed doing exceedingly more than you could ever ask or imagine.

Tim Story says that many people live an "almost life" because they have an "at most mentality". At most has a limit. If you have an at most mentality, then you believe there is a limit on God's blessing, a limit on your influence, but our God is not a God of limits. There are no limits with God. In Mark 9:23, Jesus says,

"Anything is possible if a person believes." (NLT)

I read about a study that was done where scientists took fleas and put them in a jar and then put a lid over the top. The fleas would jump and continually hit the lid. They must have decided that didn't feel very good, because after a period of time, they would jump almost to the top of the ceiling of the jar.

After this, they took the lid off the jar and let the fleas out. Even with the lid off, those fleas would continue to jump only as high as the jar. They had been conditioned to believe they had a limit.

How sad it is when Christians live this way. How sad when we allow our circumstances to define us and condition us into thinking there are limits to the height we can go with God. God wants to bless you and use you; He wants to see you live out your purpose and live out an incredible legacy.

Don't ever allow your circumstances to define what's possible. When God is on the throne of your life and you are committed to serving Him, nothing is impossible. Get rid of the "at most mentality" and exchange it for an "utmost mentality".

God has his utmost in store for you.

Action Points

1. Describe a time when you exercised faith in a difficult situation.

   _____

   _____

   _____

   _____

2. Which acronym of F.E.A.R. best describes you? What fears are holding you back from pursuing your dreams? What can you do today to face those fears and rise above them?

   _____

   _____

   _____

   _____

3. Is there an area in your life where you have made progress and are _almost_ there? What keeps you persevering so you don't give up?

   _____

   _____

   _____

   _____

PART 3
Fix Your Focus

7

Focus On Your Purpose

"The two most important days in your life are the day you are born and the day you find out why."
– Mark Twain

One day, the great Hank Aaron went up to bat while legendary catcher Yogi Berra was behind the plate. Yogi was known for taunting batters and trying his best to distract them while in the batter's box.

On this one particular occasion, while Hank was at the plate, Yogi said, "Hey Hank! You're holding the bat wrong. You have to be able to read the writing on the bat. It's facing the wrong way. Hank, your gonna break the bat if you can't read the writing."

Without saying anything back to Yogi, Hank just stared straight ahead, focusing on the baseball as it left the pitcher's hand. Hank saw the ball, swung the bat, and hit the ball out of the park for a home run.

Hank ran around the bases and after crossing home plate, continued towards the dugout. He stopped about half way, turned around and said to Yogi, "Hey Yogi! I didn't come here to read!"

Yogi knew why he was there and what he was supposed to do.

If you don't know your purpose, there will be voices to distract you and confuse you; this is a part of being intentional. Knowing your purpose is essential to living out the legacy you want to leave and you have to be able to block out the many voices around you that will try to distract you.

Earlier, we talked about the importance of fortifying our foundation on Jesus Christ. Then in part 2 we looked at understanding what faith is and the importance of feeding our faith daily. Part 3 of this book will teach you how to know and stay focused on your purpose.

What is your purpose?

It's important you know the answer to this question. God created you on purpose, for a purpose. You will come up short every time if you don't passionately pursue what God has planned for you.

Zack Ertz is a tight end for the Super Bowl Champions, Philadelphia Eagles. He said, "Our number one goal on this Earth is to make disciples. That's the only job we want to do. We want to draw people to Jesus."

Zack's job is a football player in the NFL but that's not his purpose.

He understands his purpose is bigger than his job and his job is simply a means for God to use him to impact others.

The same is true for you. Your job is not your purpose, but a vehicle so Christ can use you to touch as many lives as possible.

Hebrews 12:1-2a gives us some excellent instruction and encouragement when it comes to purpose. In this passage, I want us to look closely at four things we can learn and apply to living out our purpose:

Therefore, since we are surrounded by such a great cloud of witnesses, let us throw off everything that hinders and the sin that so easily entangles and let us run with perseverance the race marked out for us. Let us fix our eyes on Jesus. Hebrews 12:1-2a (NIV)

There are four things this verse tells us about our purpose.

1. Run Your Race

The Scripture says to run **"the race marked out for us"**. The first thing you have to know is that God really does have a special, unique purpose for your life. There is a race for you and me to run. In chapter 1, we talked about passing the baton, and how if we don't run our race well, there will be no baton to pass. If you don't stay on course, you're going to leave your legacy falling short.

When we accept the race that God has marked out for us, we are able to live our lives to the fullest. The worst thing you can do is resist it or, even worse, just say no to it.

There are probably things about your race you don't like and that you wish you could change. I believe we should do everything possible to make the best possible life for ourselves and our families, but it must fit within the will of God. The more you seek Him and the more you focus on God's purpose, the more He will reveal it to you.

You have to spend time with the Lord discovering what the race is He has set for you. As you read in chapter 4, it took me a couple of years to really understand what my purpose is and my purpose has evolved over time. In my first 10-15 years of teaching and coaching, my purpose was to influence as many people as I could within that arena. While this was taking place, unbeknownst to me, God was slowly preparing me for this phase of my life right now. He was preparing me for a whole new ministry and influence that I was not ready for 20 years ago.

I believe God is always preparing us. At the same time, He wants to use us right where we are. We must make the most of every situation we are currently in, but also understand everything we go through is preparation for the future. Sometimes we have no idea that what we are currently going through is training ground for the future.

Just keep running your race. Be consistent and stay focused.

In the next chapter, we're going to look at how to have discipline so that we stay on course. It's easy to lose focus but our legacy demands that we keep on running.

Many years ago, the LA Times reported on an NCAA cross-country meet where 123 of the 128 runners were disqualified for getting off course. Somewhere along the way, there was confusion about which direction to go and 123 competitors took a wrong turn. Those runners continued to run but they were running the wrong race!

Sometimes the course is well marked and other times we need to slow down and make sure we haven't got off track. Staying grounded in the Word of God and keeping our minds fixed on Him will help ensure we stay on the right path.

2. Run with Perseverance

Not only are we to run the race that's been marked out for us, but we are to run it with perseverance. The passage above says, **"…and let us run with perseverance the race marked out for us…"**

It's a grind! It's a marathon not a sprint. The Christian life is not easy and we must understand that and expect it to be difficult at times.

Sticking with your purpose will require perseverance. The greater your purpose, the greater Satan will work to defeat you. His game plan is to keep you from living out your purpose but you must stand strong, keep running, and never give up.

Remind yourself that there will always be ups and downs, highs and lows. Just know it and expect it.

The big question you must ask yourself is, "How bad do I want it?" If you want it bad enough, then you will have the perseverance and the endurance to stick it out. If you don't really want it bad enough, then you'll quit when the going gets tough.

Your purpose will provide passion and passion will enable you to persevere.

I first heard a story about a young man who wanted to be successful from John Maxwell over 25 years ago. Since then, Eric Thomas has told the story and through it, has impacted millions with his message of "as bad as you want to breathe" and "Breathe University". Even if you've heard it before, it's still a great story that will make you ask yourself, "How bad do I really want to live out the legacy God has for me?"

A young man wanted to be successful and so he went to the guru in the village where he lived. The guru was the wisest man in the land and everyone looked to him for answers.

The young man went to him and said, "I really want to be successful. Will you show me how?"

The guru looked him up and down and said, "You want to be successful, huh? Ok. Meet me at the beach tomorrow morning at 6:00am."

The young man showed up the next morning on time. The guru asked him, "What is it you want?"

He replied, "More than anything, I want to be successful."

The guru said, "Ok", then took him to the edge of the water. They waded out into the ocean and got about neck deep; the young man had to stand on his tip-toes to keep his head above water.

The guru asked him again what it is he wanted, and the young man said as before, "I want to be successful!"

Immediately the guru put his hands on the young man and shoved him under the water. He held him under for 10 seconds...20 seconds...30 seconds.

He let him up and he began coughing and gasping for air. He asked him again what he wanted and he answered the same as before, "I want to be successful." No sooner had he got the words out of his mouth had the guru shoved him under again.

This time, 30 seconds went by...then 40 seconds...then 50 seconds...finally after a full minute, he let the man up and he again was coughing and wheezing and gasping for air. The guru asked him the same question as before, "What is it you want?"

This time, all the young man could say was, "Air! I want air!"

The guru looked at him and said, "When you want to be successful as bad as you want air, then you will be successful."

When you want to run your race as badly as you want air to breathe, then you will do it. You will find a way to persevere. The problem with most people is they don't want it bad enough. They only want it if things are in their favor but as soon as something goes wrong, they give up on it.

If you don't know your purpose but want to discover it as bad as you want to breathe, eventually you will know it. God is faithful and if you do everything He says to do, He will reveal Himself to you.

Matthew 6:33 says,

"Seek the Kingdom of God above all else, and live righteously, and he will give you everything you need." (NLT)

And Proverbs 3:6 tells us,

"Seek his will in all you do, and he will show you which path to take." (NLT)

There will be plenty of times in life when things are not in your favor. There will be times when you question your calling and don't know exactly what to do. But if you continually seek God above everything else, He will provide what you need in the right time and in the right way.

How bad do you want it?

3. Throw Off The Things That Hinder

You can't run your race hanging on to the baggage that God wants you to get rid of. You can try, but until you address the things in your life that are hindering you, you will simply come up short. You will never live out your purpose until that baggage is gone.

"Throw off everything that hinders and the sin that so easily entangles." (NIV)

We all have things in our lives that weigh us down. There are things that trip us up and keep us from being the person that God wants us to be. But we must throw these things off. Get rid of them as quickly as possible. To me, "Throw off" means I need to get it as far away from me as possible.

What is in your life that you need to throw off? Are you willing to get rid of it? Maybe it's a bad relationship, maybe it's a habit, an addiction, an attitude, maybe it's something that's been a part of your life for a long time.

Perhaps there's something you've thrown off but you've picked it back up again – God is telling you today that you need to get it out of your life once and for all.

Sometimes an athlete will train with a weighted vest on. They will do running, jumping, and sprinting exercises wearing a special vest that weighs 30-40 pounds. With the vest on, they are not capable of performing to their full capabilities; it slows them down. They would never wear it in actual competition because it would keep them from being effective. But they wear it as a training aid.

It's an interesting experience when the athlete takes the vest off. All of a sudden, there's freedom they had not experienced with it on. The weight has been lifted and they are now able to do things in a way they couldn't before.

What a difference it makes when the weights come off.

Too many Christians are trying to live a Godly life with a weighted vest on. They are weighed down by their sin, their anger, their egos, their selfishness, their addictions, their habits, and they will never be able to run their race effectively until they throw off these things that are hindering them.

Sometimes they wear it for so long they forget it's there and think it's a normal part of life. My friend, it's not supposed to be that way. That's not how God intended your life to be. If you stop and obey the Holy Spirit and get those things out of your life that He has been talking to you about, you will find freedom and peace like you've never known before.

4. Fix Your Eyes on Jesus

The final thing this passage tells us is to, **"Fix your eyes on Jesus"**.

This is where it all starts. He is the target. He is the goal, the finish line. He is the one we are trying to pattern our lives after, so we must fix our focus on Him.

The word "focus" is both a noun and a verb. If you look it up in the dictionary, here's what you'll find:

1. *the center of interest or activity. Also, an act of concentrating interest or activity on something.*
2. *the state or quality of having and producing clear visual definition.*

This is the type of focus we should have on Christ. He should be at the center of our interest and activities. With this type of focus, you will know and live out your purpose but you can't allow yourself to get distracted.

The world is full of distractions, like Yogi Berra taunting Hank

Aaron, the voices that try to distract you from your purpose are everywhere. I call them WMD's: *Weapons of Mass Distraction*. Be aware of them in your life and don't let them pull you off course.

Many years ago, I went with my dad to watch the Sacramento Kings at Arco Arena. At the end of the game, the King's had a one-point lead with one second to go. However, the King's had committed a foul and the other team was awarded two free throws.

As the player from the opposing team stepped up to the line, the crowd of over 10,000 people understood what was at stake. If this player made one free throw it would mean overtime. If he made both of them, it would mean a loss for the home team. If the player missed the free throws, however, it would mean a victory for the Kings.

The referee handed him the ball and the fans in that arena became deafening. They yelled at the top of their voices in an attempt to distract the player from making the free throws.

In addition to the noise, behind the backboard were crazy fans jumping up and down, waving their arms back and forth in the direct line of sight of the player. As he lifted his arms to shoot the ball, the fans screamed even louder.

In what seemed like slow motion, the ball headed to the rim and swished in.

The score was now tied.

Knowing the game was really on the line now, the fans were

somehow even louder than before. In the midst of all the incredible distractions, the player sunk the second free throw, giving his team the victory and the Kings a loss.

While we were in the car driving home, we turned on the radio to listen to the post-game interviews. The reporters asked the player who made the winning free throws how he did it, "How were you able to focus and make those shots in the midst of all the chaos and distractions?"

His response was insightful. He said, "I just focused in on the rim. Even though I knew the crowd was there, I didn't really hear them. I was just locked in on the target."

That's how we must live — so focused on Jesus, our target, that we don't even notice the distractions and temptations are all around us.

Remember this, you won't get rid of the distractions and temptations in your life. They will always be there in some form and the more you live out your purpose, the more Satan is going to fight against you. But the key is being so focused, so locked into Jesus Christ, that the distractions become much less prevalent in your life.

Action Points

1. Describe in two or three sentences what your purpose is.

_____

_____

_____

_____

_____

2. If you are unsure of your purpose, think about these questions: What are you good at? What brings you joy? Who are the people in your life you have influence on? Your purpose will be wrapped up in these answers. Begin to ask God to show you what your purpose is and how you can live it out each and every day.

_____

_____

_____

_____

_____

3. What is the most difficult thing you are working through right now? What will it take to persevere in the midst of this difficult situation?

_____

_____

_____

_____

_____

_____

4. Think of the weighted vest analogy. Is there anything in your life that the vest represents that you need to throw off?

_____

_____

_____

_____

_____

5. How can you be more focused on Christ and give less attention to the distractions?

_____

_____

_____

_____

_____

8

2 Keys To Staying Focused

F.O.C.U.S. = Follow One Course Until Success

"...dear brothers and sisters...I focus on this one thing: Forgetting the past and looking forward to what lies ahead."
– Philippians 3:14 (NLT)

I often use the acronym F.O.C.U.S. which means "Follow One Course Until Success" to help me stay focused on different projects until I have them completed. I have to admit, I have been known to start something, then jump to something else, then to something else, and keep jumping around to different things not completing anything! My mind easily wonders and gets distracted.

The one course we should follow more than any other is to love like Christ loves. There are two keys to keeping your focus fixed on Jesus. We must have:

1. Congruency

2. Love

Congruency

Congruency is a term often used in geometry when describing two shapes that are exactly the same. This is not only a geometry word, however, this is a word that we must apply to our lives as Christians. There must be congruency between what we say and what we do. They need to be exactly the same.

If you say:

- Being healthy is important to you but you eat junk food all the time, then being healthy is not really important to you.
- Your kids and family are your priority but you never spend time with them, then they are not your priority.
- Living within your means is important to you but you keep overspending every month and keep getting further in debt, then it's not really that important to you.
- You love Jesus but don't spend any time with Him, then you don't really love Him as much as you say.

It's easy to say something is important, but it's not your words that determine if it really is or not. The proof is in your actions. Every single time.

Congruency in our lives is essential to living out a Godly legacy. If your words don't match up with your actions, you're missing the mark.

Now, we get congruency when *integrity* intersects with *discipline*.

Integrity

Integrity is who we are when no one is looking. A tough question for us to wrestle with is, "Who am I when no one is around?" Am I the same person when in the presence of others?

Some people are far too concerned with how they are perceived by others. But your focus should be on building your character; integrity is achieved when you are more concerned with your character than you are with your reputation.

The great Coach John Wooden said, "Be more concerned with your character than your reputation because your character is what you really are while your reputation is merely what others think you are."

James 1:6-8 says,

"Do not waver, for a person with divided loyalty is as unsettled as a wave of the sea that is blown and tossed by the wind. Such people should not expect to receive anything from the Lord. Their loyalty is divided between God and the world, and they are unstable in everything they do." (NLT)

If you are divided in your heart, you will be unstable. If you are unstable, you will say one thing and do another. An undivided heart brings about a lack of integrity every time.

Integrity is essential but we take our influence to a new level when we also have discipline.

Discipline

Discipline is the other key ingredient to living a congruent life. The best way to stay focused on Christ is to combine integrity and discipline.

For years, I have taught the definition of discipline is: "Doing what you have to do, when you have to do it, whether you feel like it or not."

Notice this involves three things; first, is *knowing* what you have to do. I have met people who are so overwhelmed with life, they don't even know what to do. The first key to discipline is knowing what to do. But for most of us, this is not the issue – we know what we should do, we just don't do it.

The second part is *doing* it when you have to do it. I know that some people are very good at procrastinating and have been doing it for years. But when you learn to do things the moment they should be and could be done, you will find life is much, much easier. The problem is, we don't do things because we don't feel like it.

This takes us to the third part. Discipline requires you to act independently of how you *feel*. If we only did the things we felt like doing, we wouldn't get very far in life. Without discipline life may be fun...for a time, but then it would catch up to you.

The goal with discipline is to sacrifice what you want at the moment for what you really want most. If you are able to do this on a daily basis, then you are a disciplined person, able to make the decisions that will bring about the results in your life that you really want.

Take this concept of discipline and combine it with integrity. This is the person who is focused on Christ, running a great race, and living out a great legacy.

Love

The second thing we must have in order to keep focused on Jesus is love.

Love is where it's at!

Love is one of those things that's easy to say yet, oftentimes, very hard to live out. It's easy to love when you are loved back, but what about when it's not reciprocated? What about when you are being treated unfairly? Living out the unconditional love of Christ in your marriage, your job, in all your relationships and interactions is very difficult.

When we really love like Christ, we love completely independently of what the other person says or does.

I Corinthians 13:13 says,

"Three things will last forever--faith, hope, and love--and the greatest of these is love." (NLT)

If love is the greatest, you cannot leave a great legacy without love being part of the equation. Love must be rooted in who we are and how we live.

If you implement everything I've written about in this book but do not have love, then you've missed it! Without love, our legacy is hollow and meaningless. Love must be at the core of all we do.

So how do we achieve this?

Philippians 2:3-4 gives us a great start. It says,

"Don't be selfish; don't try to impress others. Be humble, thinking of others as better than yourselves. Don't look out only for your own interests, but take an interest in others, too." (NLT)

Now, you may be thinking, "What? Think of others as better than myself?" This is not easy, but this is what Christ is calling us to do.

I Corinthians 13:2 says,

"If I had the gift of prophecy, and if I understood all of God's secret plans and possessed all knowledge, and if I had such faith that I could move mountains, but didn't love others, I would be nothing." (NLT)

You can do all kinds of great things in the world, even move mountains, but if you do not love others you are nothing. Love is essential to leaving a Godly legacy!

I Corinthians 13 is known as the love chapter. In verses 4-8, it describes what love is,

"Love is patient, love is kind. It does not envy, it does not boast, it is not proud. It does not dishonor others, it is not self-seeking,

it is not easily angered, it keeps no record of wrongs. Love does not delight in evil but rejoices with the truth. It always protects, always trusts, always hopes, always perseveres. Love never fails." I Corinthians 13:4-8 (NIV)

I want you to do something. Go back and read that passage again, but this time insert your name where it says, "Love". So, for me I read, "Gary is patient, Gary is kind. Gary does not envy…" etc. If you can, go somewhere alone and read it aloud.

As you read that, how did you feel?

I have done this many times and each time I feel like a failure because I know this is not who I am. However, I know I am becoming more and more like this every day because this is my focus. I read the passage this way as an affirmation of who I am trying to become.

Living this way, with this type of love at the core of who we are is what Christ has called us to do. It's a process of learning and growing in His love.

Action Points

1. On a scale of 1 to 10, how congruent are you? A 10 is your words and actions match up perfectly. A 1 means they are not at all the same.

   _____

2. Do you agree with the definition of discipline? Why or why not? In what ways do you need to exercise more discipline in your life?

   _____

   _____

   _____

   _____

3. Read I Corinthians 13:4-8 over and over, inserting your name. This is your declaration and affirmation of who you are in Christ. You won't be perfect and may be far from it. But this is your heart's desire and you are going to keep it at the forefront of your mind. Read it again aloud and boldly speak the words of life and love into your heart and soul.

   _____

   _____

   _____

   _____

PART 4
Finish Strong

9

It Doesn't Happen Overnight

"Patience is not just the ability to wait, but the ability to keep a good attitude while you are waiting."
– Joyce Meyer

"Hardships often prepare ordinary people for an extraordinary destiny."
– C.S. Lewis

If you plant a Chinese Bamboo seed, water it, fertilize it, cultivate it, and weed around it for an entire year, nothing will happen. For an entire year, you will see no visible signs that anything is actually happening to that seed.

If you continue to water and cultivate it for a second year, by the time you get to the end of the year you will still see no signs of life in that seed.

If you continue watering and nurturing that seed for a third year, and a fourth year, and even a fifth year, nothing at all will happen on the surface.

However, after the five-year mark, it will grow over 80 feet in six weeks!

Sometimes life is like a Chinese Bamboo seed. We work, we give everything we've got, but we don't see results. The key is staying faithful. The key is staying with what you know is right, even when it doesn't seem to be working.

As you determine to live out your legacy, there will be times when you think you're not making a difference. As we've talked about throughout this book, you cannot give up. You must be patient, keep going, and FINISH STRONG!

Your legacy is not established in a day, a week, a month, or even a year. Your legacy is established over the course of your lifetime. It's what you do day in and day out.

John Maxwell says it's not what you do in a day that counts, but what you do *daily*.

Perhaps you're in a place right now where you've been trying to live right, you know you need to be living for God, but things just don't seem to be working out. Maybe you're at a place where you're wondering if you are really making your life count. My encouragement to you is to keep going. Keep believing that you are making a difference and that God is using your life right now, right where you are.

A big problem in today's society is that things are so immediately available. You can send or receive money in a moment, you can

THE LEGACY GAME PLAN

make a purchase online and Amazon will have it to you the next day, and Google provides any information you need in a fraction of a second.

I love the advancement of technology, but we have to remember that our legacy is not instantaneous. There are still some things in life that take a long time and I'm afraid too many in this upcoming generation do not fully understand this.

Be an I Can Christian

A very popular scripture is Philippians 4:13. It says,

"For I can do everything through Christ, who gives me strength." (NLT)

I want to encourage you to finish strong each and every day with this great verse.

This passage says "...I can do..."

Now, it's Christ's strength that supplies the power, but this verse says it is "I" who is "doing". Sometimes we want God to fight our battles for us and there are times He will. But sometimes He wants us to step up and fight.

My friend and former Pastor, Mel Rich, likes to say from this verse, "I CAN be a Christian...I CAN be forgiven...I CAN have a great marriage...I CAN be the person God wants me to be...I CAN leave a great legacy...I CAN be a spiritual champion."

I CAN through Christ's strength, is a powerful message and a powerful way to live. I heard a speaker years ago say that the four letters in "I Can" make an acronym and it has stuck with me for almost 30 years. As we get ready to close out this book, I want you to determine to fight the good fight and persevere in the race that God has marked out for you.

Here's what "I CAN" stands for:

I – Imagination
I Corinthians 2:9 says,

"...**No eye has seen, no ear has heard, and no mind has imagined what God has prepared for those who love him." (NLT)**

As you run your race strong to the finish line, imagine the great things God has in store for you. If you use all your imagination and try to think of the most amazing things God could do in your life, you will still fall short of what He has in store.

Dream big!

How does God want to use you in ministry? What is that dream you have deep inside that you keep thinking about? God wants you to live large. He wants you, your family, your church, and your influence to be at the top of your game.

I love the story of Walt Disney. Walt built Disneyland in Southern California and then he decided he wanted to do the same thing on the East Coast. So, he began to build Disney World in Florida. Unfortunately, Walt passed away before Disney World was completed.

When Walt passed away, his brother took over the project and saw the completion of Disney World. On the grand opening day, there was a great celebration. People came from all over and enjoyed this magnificent place.

Walt's brother stood off to the side where he could just take it all in. It was in that moment that a lady walked up to Walt's brother and said, "Isn't it a shame that Walt couldn't be here to see this?"

He looked at her and said, "Ma'am, it's because Walt saw it that it's here today."

I don't know where you are in your life, but God has more in store for you. However, it will not come to pass unless you can see it and believe it. You have to believe that God can do it but you also have to see the possibilities in your own mind.

C – Commitment

You have to have commitment to living out a Godly legacy and fulfilling His purpose for you.

Philippians 3:14 says,

"I press on to reach the end of the race and receive the heavenly prize for which God, through Christ Jesus, is calling us." (NLT)

A part of being an "I Can Christian" is being committed. There is a world of difference between being committed and being interested. Many people are interested in losing weight and getting in shape but they are not committed to it. Many people are interested in success but they are not committed to it. Many people are interested in having a better marriage but they are not committed to it.

Unfortunately, many people are interested in Jesus but they are not committed.

Ken Blanchard has this to say about it, "There's a difference between interest and commitment. When you're interested in something you do it only when it's convenient. When you're committed to something, you accept no excuses, only results."

In the Face of Criticism

It's hard to stay committed when you face obstacles and criticism. When things are going well, when people are supporting you and patting you on the back, it's easy to stay focused and committed. But you have to ask yourself if you are committed even when the road is difficult and there are haters questioning and criticizing you.

Will you let them deter you or motivate you?

I love this famous quote by Teddy Roosevelt, delivered in a speech on April 23, 1910:

"It's not the critic who counts; not the man who points out how the strong man stumbles, or where the doer of deeds could have done them better. The credit belongs to the man who is in the arena, whose face is marred by dust and sweat and blood; who strives valiantly; who errs, who comes up short again and again, because there is no effort without error and shortcoming; but who does

actually strive to do the deeds; who knows great enthusiasms, the great devotions; who spends himself in a worthy cause; who at the best knows in the end the triumph of high achievement, and who at the worst, if he fails, at least fails while daring greatly, so that his place shall never be with those cold and timid souls who neither know victory nor defeat."

The fact you are reading this book tells me you want to dare greatly! Don't allow the critics and naysayers to keep you from achieving your dreams and living out the legacy God has intended for you to live.

A-Attitude

Attitude is a little thing that makes a huge difference. But what should your attitude be like?

Philippians 2:5 tells us exactly. It says,

"You must have the same attitude that Christ Jesus had." (NLT)

That pretty much sums it up when it comes to your attitude.

Jesus is the standard and we are commanded in Scripture to have His attitude. Will it always happen? Probably not. But it is still the standard. When we mess up, we have to get right back to the mindset of Christ and every day work to be more like Him. It all starts with our attitude.

Take a minute and examine your attitude towards life, towards your circumstances, towards your relationships, and towards your legacy.

Chuck Swindoll's words on attitude have been repeated many times, but it's worth repeating here because it is so true. He says:

"The longer I live, the more I realize the impact of attitude on life. Attitude, to me, is more important than facts. It is more important than the past, than education, than money, than circumstances, than failures, than successes, than what other people think, say or do. It is more important than appearance, giftedness or skill. It will make or break a company... a church... a home. The remarkable thing is we have a choice every day regarding the attitude we embrace for that day. We cannot change our past... we cannot change the fact that people will act in a certain way. We cannot change the inevitable. The only thing we can do is play the one string we have, and that is our attitude... I am convinced that life is 10% what happens to me and 90% how I react to it. And so it is with you... we are in charge of our Attitudes."

Attitude is a Choice

The crazy thing about attitude is that we get to choose it. It's not forced upon us, it's a choice we make every single day.

Victor Frankl survived the Nazi Concentration camps. He had everything taken away from him; he literally had the clothes on his back stripped from him, his wedding ring taken, and his family was killed. He endured the worst conditions a human can face.

Yet, in spite of what he went through, he said, "The one thing you can't take away from me is the way I choose to respond to what you do to me. The last of one's freedoms is to choose one's attitude in any given circumstance."

We always choose our attitude in any situation.

N – Never Give Up

Winston Churchill said, "Never, never, never give up!"

We've talked already about persevering and running our race even when it's uphill. A favorite verse of mine reminds me to not give up because we will eventually get there.

I talked earlier about Galatians 6:9, which says,

"So let's not get tired of doing what is good. At just the right time we will reap a harvest of blessing if we don't give up." (NLT)

Giving up is just one thing we cannot do.

Thomas Edison said, "Many times life's failures are those people who did not realize how close they were to success when they gave up."

If there's one thing I want you to understand from this book about your life and legacy, it's that you cannot give up. As hard as things may be with your spouse, with your kids, your finances, your job, and with all the things we face in life, you cannot give up.

There's too much at stake. God has so much in store for you and for those who will be inspired by your legacy.

I = imagination
C = commitment
A = attitude
N = never give up

Action Points

1. What dream do you have that you are currently pursuing? Do you really believe that God can bring it about?

   _____

   _____

   _____

   _____

   _____

   _____

2. How would you describe your commitment to Jesus? Are you truly committed to Him or are you just interested in Him?

   _____

   _____

   _____

   _____

   _____

   _____

3. Are there areas in your life where you need to change your attitude? If so, will you?

   _____

   _____

   _____

   _____

_____

_____

4. Read Galatians 6:9 again and think about some of the good things you have done in the past. What was the harvest? What is one thing you are doing now that you are tempted to give up on? What will the harvest be if you do not give up?

_____

_____

_____

_____

_____

_____

10
Your Lasting Legacy

"The greatest legacy one can pass on to one's children and grandchildren is not money or other material things accumulated in one's life, but rather a legacy of character and faith."
— Billy Graham

"How you use the opportunities you're given to affect world around you will determine the legacy you leave behind."
— Tony Dungy

In this final chapter, I want you to create your game plan. In the pages that follow, you will write out four things you need to come back to again and again. This is the beginning of your Legacy Game Plan.

Legacy Statement

First, is your legacy statement. Think about the things you've read in this book and what's really important to you. Think about what God is calling you to do and the race He has marked out for you. As you write your legacy statement, remember this is a declaration and affirmation about how you are going to live each and every day. Your legacy statement will inspire you when you're tempted to fall away and guide you when you face uncertainty. Read this statement along with your legacy prayer every morning and every night.

Below is my legacy statement, that I first wrote on September 23, 2015:

"If my life inspires my kids to go for greatness in everything they do, then I did not live in vain. When I am gone, if they and others can use my life as motivation to just go for it, to hold nothing back and chase their dreams with everything they've got, then my life will have accomplished something worthwhile. And most importantly, if my life was able to point them to Jesus and, because of how I lived, thing things I said, and the choices I made, they choose to follow Him with all their heart, then my life will have been well lived."

What Is Your Legacy Statement? Write it down now:

_____

_____

_____

_____

_____

_____

_____

_____

Legacy Prayer

Next is your Legacy prayer. This is a specific prayer to the Lord asking Him for strength, guidance, perseverance, and a continued desire to live out your legacy statement. You know you better than anyone. You know where you are weak and in what areas you will need the most help. Take a minute and write out your legacy prayer and then pray this prayer every morning when you wake up and every night when you go to bed.

The following is my legacy prayer:

Lord, use me to reach people and make a difference for you. Allow my influence to reach beyond anything I could imagine and use my life to make a difference in others. May it begin first and foremost at home with my own family. Let me be inspiring and motivating so that others go for their greatness and chase their dreams and find the purpose you have for them.

What Is Your Legacy Prayer? Write it down now:

_____

_____

_____

_____

_____

_____

_____

_____

Tombstone Testimony

Your tombstone testimony is one brief sentence that sums up your life. It's short so it could fit on a tombstone. One day, we will breathe our last breath. When you're gone, what will you want people to be able to read about you, in one sentence, that gives them a glimpse into your legacy?

My Tombstone Testimony is:

"Here lies Gary Greeno, a man who made a difference."

What Is Your Tombstone Testimony? Write it down now:

_____

_____

Life Verse

Now I want you to identify a life verse. For me, during the experiences I've had in life, the Lord has brought one specific verse to me over and over again. However, if you have more than one, that's ok.

My life verse is James 1:12. It says,

"Blessed is the man who perseveres under trial because, having stood the test, that person will receive the crown of life that the Lord has promised to those who love him." (BSB)

This verse became very meaningful to me in the early 1990s. I attended Olive Knolls Church of the Nazarene in Bakersfield, CA, during a new building project. They were building a new gym/sanctuary and one Sunday morning, Pastor Mel Rich had the congregation go to the new building and had them write their favorite verse somewhere on the frame of the new structure.

It symbolized that the building belonged to the Lord and everything that would be done in that place was only because of the powerful Word of God.

I wrote down James 1:12. I was in my 20's at the time and had no idea of the trials and difficulties that I would encounter over the next 30 years. Even today, I have no idea what trials lie ahead for me, but this I do know: the promise of James 1:12 will not let me down.

What is your life verse? Write it in the space provided and memorize it if you haven't already. Know this "go-to" verse will always be there for you.

What Is Your Life Verse? Write it down now:

_____
_____
_____
_____
_____
_____
_____
_____

Now you have your game plan in place! Your game plan will guide you and serve as a roadmap when making decisions.

Now, it's time to execute.

Read your legacy statement every day. Remember, this is your affirmation that you are going to live out the legacy that you want to leave daily. This is who you are and what you want. It's time to make it a reality. Pray your legacy prayer daily. As you do this,

God will empower you to intentionally live it out.

James 5:16 says,

"The prayer of a righteous person is powerful."

And in Romans 8:11 it says,

"The Spirit of God, who raised Jesus from the dead, lives in you. And just as God raised Christ Jesus from the dead, he will give life to your mortal bodies by this same Spirit living within you." (NLT)

Remember, the same power that raised Jesus from the dead is available to you. Allow that power to rise up inside of you as you execute your legacy game plan.

Executing your game plan will make you unstoppable. It doesn't mean you will never stumble or experience defeat, but it does mean you can rise up every time you fall. And that's really what being unstoppable is – not allowing anything to stop you from giving life the absolute best you have to give.

Keep your tombstone testimony at the forefront of your mind, and memorize your life verse so it becomes a part of who you are at your core.

I would also suggest going back through your action points regularly. As you put these action points into place, you will experience growth and enjoy looking back at them over time to see just how far you've come.

Final Words

In the 1968 Olympics, John Stephen Akhwari, an athlete from the country of Tanzania, competed in the Olympic Marathon in Mexico City, Mexico. There were 75 competitors from 41 countries in the marathon event.

The winning time was 2:20:26 by Mamo Wolde of Ethiopia. When John Stephen Akhwari entered the stadium for his final lap of the marathon, Wolde had crossed the finish line over an hour before. The sun had gone down, most of the fans in the stadium were gone and everyone else had already finished.

When Akhwari entered the stadium, he was limping, his leg bandaged and barely able to walk, much less run. During the race, he had fallen and sustained a gash in his leg and a dislocated knee. Nonetheless, he continued on; 18 of his competitors did not finish and he was not going to be number 19, even though if he did give up, everyone would have understood.

As he limped around the track, the few spectators that were remaining stood to their feet to cheer him on.

After the race, reporters gathered around him and asked him why he continued on? His response was, "My country did not send me 5,000 miles to start this race. My country sent me 5,000 miles to finish the race."

God did not create you, save you, and give you a purpose to start your race. He did it so you could finish. You may be wounded and barely able to take a step, but remember, what God calls you to, He will see you through.

Keep running, my friend, and don't ever give up!

The time to live out your legacy is now. You've got what it takes.

About The Author

Gary is a professional keynote speaker, accomplished coach and educator. Gary has been an educator and basketball coach since 1991 and has been speaking for over 10 years. He is active in his church, Horizon Christian Fellowship in Stockton, CA, where he served in 2017 as the senior interim pastor for 9 months.

Gary lives in Stockton where he coached the varsity basketball team at Lincoln High School from 2006-2019 and still teaches math. He is married to his wife, Dena, of 16 years, and has five children, Bret 26, Brittney 22, Brooke 19, Grace 15, and Luke 14.

You can follow Gary and subscribe to his motivational newsletter at www.garygreeno.com.

To contact Gary for speaking engagements, email info@garygreeno.com.

Made in the USA
Middletown, DE
22 February 2024

49687069R00076